DAVID EDGAR

David Edgar was born in 1948 into a theatre family. After a period in journalism, he took up writing full time in 1972. In 1989, he founded Britain's first graduate playwriting course, at the University of Birmingham, where he was a professor until 1999.

His original stage plays include *Death Story* (Birmingham Repertory Theatre, 1972), *Destiny* (1976: John Whiting Award) and *Maydays* (1983: Plays and Players play of the year), both for the Royal Shakespeare Company, *Entertaining Strangers* (Dorchester Community Play, 1985, then National Theatre, 1987), *That Summer* (Hampstead Theatre, London, 1987), *The Shape of the Table* (National Theatre, 1990), *Pentecost* (Royal Shakespeare Company, 1994–5: Evening Standard Best Play) and *Albert Speer* (scheduled for the National Theatre, 2000). His stage adaptations include Albie Sachs' *Jail Diary* (Royal Shakespeare Company, 1978), Mary Barnes and Joe Berke's *Mary Barnes* (Royal Court, London, 1979), a multi-award-winning version of Dickens' *Nicholas Nickleby* (Royal Shakespeare Company in London and New York, 1980–1, subsequently Channel 4) and Stevenson's *Dr Jekyll and Mr Hyde* (Royal Shakespeare Company, 1991, revised for Birmingham Rep, 1996).

David Edgar has also written several plays for the BBC (most recently *Vote for Them* and *Buying a Landslide* for television and *A Movie Starring Me* and *Talking to Mars* for radio), the biographical *Citizen Locke* for Channel 4 and the film *Lady Jane* for Paramount. He writes and reviews for a wide variety of journals, and has published a volume of essays on theatre and other matters (*The Second Time as Farce*, 1988).

By the same author

Destiny
Dr Jekyll and Mr Hyde
Entertaining Strangers
The Jail Diary of Albie Sachs
Mary Barnes
Nicholas Nickleby
Pentecost
Teendreams & Our Own People
That Summer
The Shape of the Table
Vote for Them
Wreckers

Edgar Plays: One (*Destiny, Mary Barnes, The Jail Diary of Albie Sachs, Saigon Rose, O Fair Jerusalem*)

Edgar Plays: Two (*Ecclesiastes, Nicholas Nickleby, Entertaining Strangers*)

Edgar Plays: Three (*Our Own People, Teendreams, Maydays, That Summer*)

Edgar: Shorts (*Blood Sports* with *Ball Boys, Baby Love, The National Theatre, The Midas Connection*)

The Second Time as Farce

Edgar: Shorts

short plays by

DAVID EDGAR

Blood Sports
with
Ball Boys

Baby Love

The National Theatre

The Midas Connection

NICK HERN BOOKS
London
www.nickhernbooks.co.uk

A Nick Hern Book

Edgar: Shorts first published in 1989 as an original paperback.
Reprinted in 2000 by Nick Hern Books Limited,
14 Larden Road, London W3 7ST

Ball Boys was originally published by Pluto Press

Blood Sports with *Ball Boys* © 1989 by David Edgar
Baby Love © 1989 by David Edgar
The National Theatre © 1989 by David Edgar
The Midas Connection © 1989 by David Edgar

Copyright in this collection *Edgar: Shorts*
© 1989 by David Edgar

Introduction copyright © 1989 by David Edgar

Front cover picture: copyright Caroline Forbes

Set in ITC New Baskerville and printed in Great Britain
by Athenaeum Press Ltd, Gateshead, Tyne and Wear

A CIP catalogue record for this book is available from the
British Library

ISBN 1-85459-051-0

Contents

Contents

To Nigel

Introduction

I began writing for the theatre in the early 70's, a period now
rightly seen as the Prague Spring of subsidy, a time when the
streets of the capital (and those of other cities) blossomed theatre
spaces in almost chokingly verdant profusion, presenting
bewilderingly various works of dramatic art at almost all hours of
day and night. In those days, it was said, it was just about
possible to write a three-to-five hander, at under an hour in
length, so dreadful that nobody at all would want to put it on.
But it wasn't easy.

Along with many other playwrights, then, I was able to cut my
teeth on the demanding but contained form of the short play. My
first London work – the two-hander *Two Kinds of Angel* – was
performed in a basement theatre (imaginatively called The
Basement Theatre) actually beneath a Greek St strip club; my
second was presented in a little theatre (eccentrically dubbed The
Little Theatre), somewhere near St Martin's Lane. From which I
was able to graduate – via productions at Edinburgh's legendary
Pool Theatre and elsewhere – to the grid of small London spaces
that were (and are) devoted to the presentation of serious new
work to the highest possible standards.

Baby Love, premiered at Leeds Playhouse, became my second
play at the Soho Poly (then as now, just round the corner from
the BBC). The play concerned the then topical issue of
babysnatching, and the extraordinary performance by Patti Love
in the lead part led to the play being televised by the BBC. *Blood
Sports* has also had a full dramaturgical life: originally a trilogy of
short plays about sport (called *Summer Sports*), the play was first
performed at the Birmingham Arts Lab in 1975. Shortly
afterwards, its last and longest scene – set in a Wimbledon locker
room and titled *Ball Boys* – started its long and happy solo career.
In 1976, however, the Bush Theatre (which had already presented
my political parodies *Tedderella* and *Dick Deterred*) asked me to
extend *Summer Sports* into a fuller evening, called *Blood Sports*, and
involving (in its first performance) the actor Simon Callow in full
jodhpured drag and director Simon Stokes doubling a dead tennis
star and a large black dog. The whole of *Blood Sports* continues to

be performed from time to time: but, on its own, the occasionally
updated *Ball Boys* remains far and away my most produced work.

Blood Sports is set among sporting losers; *The National Theatre* is
about the tattier end of the performing arts. In fact, it's about a
strip-show, and when performed at the Open Space in the
summer of 1975, a lot of its audience thought it *was* a strip show
(others thought it *was* the National Theatre, and it is moot which
sector of the audience was more disappointed). It was, of course,
like *Blood Sports*, a microcosm play; as indeed was *The Midas
Connection*, a play about gold bullion dealing, written in a week,
and broadcast live, as part of the BBC's brave if shortlived series
of live, topical plays broadcast at *The Eleventh Hour*.

It is perhaps no coincidence that these plays tend to cluster
around the 1974–5 period. In February 1974, the miners brought
down the Heath Government; in the summer of 1975, an initially
radical Wilson Government imposed wage controls if anything
more stringent than those against which the miners had so
effectively struck. In the intervening period, Nixon resigned over
Watergate, the IRA bombed Birmingham, Pol Pot declared
Cambodia's Year Zero, British inflation nudged 30% and the left
lost the Common Market referendum. The idea of a Britain (and
a West) ungovernable under the present system, but unwilling to
take the plunge into a new one, was the Zeitgeist of the times.
The theatre's response was a flush of metaphors of a declining
and decaying England – of which the enclosed are a fairly
representative sample.

Another event of that period, perhaps not sufficiently regarded
at the time, was Margaret Thatcher's election as leader of the
Conservative Party. And it might be thought that a set of plays
inspired by 70's ennui would sit ill in the resurgent 80s. But I
must confess myself struck by the continued resilience of the
notion of England as a sports field populated by offstage winners
and onstage losers; or indeed of the country as a strip-joint in
which social and personal decency bow before the chill wind of
market forces. And in *The Midas Connection* – a play written for live
television, but I think perfectly performable on the live stage – the
purest of commodity exchanges is the setting for a play about the
panic and despair of a market out of control.

David Edgar
April 1989

BLOOD SPORTS
with
BALL BOYS

Characters

ACT ONE

Scene One
SVEN

Scene Two
RALPH; OLIVER; A HUGE DOG; THE BANE

Scene Three
SPECTATOR; JACK; RON

Scene Four
PUTTER; COMMENTATOR; RUNNER

Scene Five
FRONT of HORSE; BACK of HORSE; RIDER

ACT TWO
RUPERT; ONEEYE; SVEN

The short play *Summer Sports* was first performed at the Birmingham Arts Lab on 3 July 1975, in a production directed by the author. The cast was Alan Hawkridge, Alan Hulse, and John Dowie.

Retitled *Blood Sports*, the play was presented in an extended version at the Bush Theatre, London, from 29 June 1976, in a production directed by Dusty Hughes. The cast was Derrick O'Connor, Stephen Bill, Simon Stokes and Simon Callow.

The second act of the play – titled *Ball Boys* – has been performed on its own, with (and sometimes without) Scene One as a prologue.

The part of OneEye in *Ball Boys* was written for Alan Hulse.

ACT ONE

Scene One

This scene as the audience comes in. In a spot lies the hideously mangled body of a blonde tennis player, SVEN. He has been strangled with cat-gut. Two chairs lie near him. On the tape, we hear his voice.

SVEN's *voice.* Und I remember, dat vinter. Vid Anya. Un du
beach. Und it ist cold. Und I am sayink, for our circulation,
ve must haf a svim. Und Anya ist agreeing. Und so ve are
takking all our clothes uff and runnink into du icy vaters.
Und it is being such gud fun.

But all I am şeeink, as ve are runnink and svimmink, ist du
blud.

Und I remember, too, ven I am beink trapped un du
mountain rescue hut vid Lotje. Und it ist ver cold. Und ve
are beink trapped till mornink ven du rescuers are cummink
vid du skis und snowshoes und du dogs vid du Corvoisier.
Und to tak our minds uff it ve are takking all our clothes uff
und haffing lots uf fun.

Blud. Blud. All I am seeink ist du blud.

Und I am rememberink too my first time vid Helga. Ufter
our first sauna. Out uf du sauna on to du ice-pack ve are
runnink. Ver ver ver cold. Beatink our nakkid buddies vid du
branches und du stickies vrom du black trees. Runnink
across du ice-pack. Nakkid. Buildink du snowmen und
trowink du snowballs on each udders nakkid buddies. O vat
fun we haf.

Du blud.

Und den I see him. Du man. He ist sittink on du
treestump. Vid a dark cloak und a vite face und a symbolic
expression.

He ist axing me to sit.

Und I am sittink.

Und he is axing me, do I know who he is?

Und I am saying, da, I know who he ist.

Und I am axing him, ven it must be.

Und he is sayink, it must be ven it must be.

Und he ist axink me vetter to vile avay du time I fancy a qvik rubber.

Und I am sayink, bit ve haf no pack.

Und he ist sayink, I haf a pack.

Und I am sayink, ve cunnot play because ve are only two und who ist to be dummy.

Und he ist sayink, you're du dummy, dummy.

So ve are playink. O Anya.

Und he ist dealink. Und I am pickink up my hand. Und I am strung in Hearts. Bit howiffer strung I am, he ist strunger. Und I am void in Clubs. Bit howiffer void I am, he ist voider. O Lotje.

Und he ist biddink. Und he ist sayink five Spades. Und I am sayink double, for I haf twenty points. Und he ist sayink redouble. Und I am realisink dat haffing twenty points ist no great comfort ven you're playink Contract Bridge vid du pale ferryman on du ice. O Helga.

Und he ist openink into my Clubs und I am thinkink dat I am trompink bit I am not trumpink for you cunnot be trompink ven you're playink double-suspension vid du grim reaper und anythink you do he vill just lead into your veak diamonds.

Und so I am givink him du trick.

Und du ice-pack.

Und du black pine-trees.

Und I am seeink Anya und Lotje und Helga not to mention Marja und Ingrid und Olga dancing across du ice-pack.

Und dey are dancink vid du man vid du dark cloak.

Und I am owink him many, many krona.

Und du blud.

Du blud.

Und I revoke.

Und it ist du end.

Blackout.

Scene Two

In the darkness, strange noises. The cry of birds. Wings flapping. Rather
frightening. The sounds grow. Then two dull shots, from a distance. Lights.
Three bushes on a grouse moor. RALPH, *a young man in rough clothes*
with tartan trimmings, stands with a Scottish flag. He isn't waving it. He
looks round, broodily. Pause. Enter OLIVER, *an older man with a beating*
stick. Despite their Scottish location, both men speak in more or less
impenetrable English Loamshire.

OLIVER. Ar. Monning, young Ralph, son on Rolf.

RALPH. Ar. Monning, nuncle Oliver. I bin here, win me flag, as
    you said, nuncle. I bin wevving it.

OLIVER. So's you should, Ralph. Here's tiffin, as me dam made
    us of chumping for ourn comfort.

    He tosses him sandwiches wrapped in paper. RALPH *starts to open*
    them.

    Nor yet, young Ralph. Afore tis chumping time, we'n still
    work as to bin doing.

RALPH. The beating an' the flag wevving.

OLIVER. Ar, the beating and the flagging, that I done ever year
    since past memb'ring, an' youn ne'er done afore, but now I
    bin bringing youn to do, all since yourn dear old blain died
    on the palsy this Lammas Eve, and you bint come to live an'
    lie win me an' me old dam.

RALPH. Ar, nuncle.

OLIVER. An'me a beater beating the biddies of the turf, an' you
    a flag wevving for to bin frightening the biddies award the
    guns, so as the Bane an' the Rich Folks can see 'em.

RALPH. Ar, nuncle.

OLIVER. It bin the twelfth on the eighth month on the year,
    young Ralph, an' the grouse-biddies fat an' greasy, an' the
    Rich Folks all come for to pepper 'em; here, on the land on
    our liege lord and lief, the Bane on Froth.

RALPH. Ar.

OLIVER. So I'll bin beating, Ralph.

Rather suddenly, he beats about the bushes. Nothing happens.

RALPH. Who bin they, then, the Rich Folks, nuncle Oliver?

OLIVER. Oh, they bin friends an' sucklers on the Bane. Many a pretty lord, gennlemen an' a fair smattering on Texas Oil Millionaires there be.

RALPH. An' be there many, an' much carousing an' fallolloping, nuncle Oliver?

OLIVER. Ay, there be many, an' much fallolloping, for tis the last twelfth on the eighth month as there'll be biddy-peppering on the lands on the Bane on Froth.

RALPH. An' why bin that, nuncle?

OLIVER. Why, for as how the Bane's to sell his land, for as then the men with the great hoes and the great ploughs come phut-phutting up the soil, win all their gallumphing.

RALPH. An' why's he to sell his land, then, nuncle, win all the gallumphing?

OLIVER. Why, for so as they can turn it to a Depot for the Natural Gas that's coming of the great waters cross ayond the Loch.

RALPH. Ar?

OLIVER. Ar. I'll be beating, Ralph.

Rather suddenly, he beats. A grouse flies out of the bush and exits, as RALPH *vaguely waves at it.*

RALPH. You got'un, nuncle.

OLIVER. Ar.

Pause. A HUGE DOG fallollops across the stage and out. They watch it pass.

RALPH. Nuncle.

OLIVER. Ar, Ralph son on Rolf?

RALPH. Bint it that yourn cottage be on the land on the Bane?

OLIVER. Ar, Ralph.

RALPH. An' bint it that I be living in yourn cottage on the land on the Bane, nuncle?

OLIVER. Ar.

RALPH. An' bint it that we gang be gallumphed for a Natural Gas Depot then nuncle?

OLIVER. So be't, Ralph.

Pause.

RALPH. Ar.

Pause.

Ar, nuncle?

OLIVER. Ar?

RALPH. What's bin to become on us, then, nuncle?

OLIVER. What's to bin done, young Ralph? For what is mun be, an' all that is mun be as't should.

Pause.

RALPH. Bin youn quite sure on that, nuncle?

OLIVER. Ar, Ralph. E'en on the Bane on Froth his-self, win all his works, they mun be as they should.

RALPH. Ar.

Slight pause.

OLIVER. So I'll be beating, Ralph.

He beats. A second grouse flies out, RALPH *waving vaguely. A* HUGE DOG *gallumphs across the stage. They watch it pass.*

RALPH. Ar. The Bane.

OLIVER. Ar.

RALPH. Mad Malcolm, they bin calling him, up Lunnon, so I din hear tell him called.

OLIVER. Bin calling oo?

RALPH. The Bane.

OLIVER. So may't be, Ralph son on Rolf, so may't be. But Lunnon ways bint ways on like on us.

RALPH. An' I did hear tell, nuncle, on wild nights in Lunnon, on the Bane, or Mad Malcolm as he'm called, on wild orgies ganging on past nine of hour on the clock, win all fallolloping and loose women and riding on taxicabs.

OLIVER. Ar, young Ralph, saying aught on that'll surely see youn ratcheted, yourn back well stippled come Candlemas.

RALPH. An' I bin hearing further, on tales on a yeasty young rollock, her'n called Sweet Sadie on Dagenham, who'm did bear Mad Malcolm a young grumbling what she in horror and despair did leave on the Central Line – whatever or where'n'ever that may'n be – afore flinging hernself amid the gungy waters on the Turpentine.

OLIVER. Well, an' I bin hearing naught on that, young Ralph, an I did, I'd sure as cowdung bin forgetting it, as' bin dang'rous talk, an' liable to get the teller all his just desserts.

RALPH. Ar, well, an' all on us got ourn just desserts, ay, an' Mad Malcolm too, there'd be no puddin' for any'n'us.

OLIVER. Now there'n a true thing as you'n saying, verily. Say things as that, an' leave the ways on Lunnon folk to them as kens 'em.

Pause.

RALPH. Shall youn be beating an' me wevving more'n, nuncle?

OLIVER. Nar. They'm overt Meanswood Spinney now, young Ralph, an' we can bin chumping ourn tiffin.

RALPH *sits as* OLIVER *goes towards exit.*

RALPH. Youn bint chumping nor tiffin, nuncle?

OLIVER. Nor yet, young Ralph. First, I bin gang to squeeze me adder.

OLIVER *exits,* RALPH *opens his sandwiches and starts chumping. A few moments. Then he notices the paper the sandwiches are wrapped in. He uncrumples it, smooths it out. It's a newspaper.*

RALPH. Writting. On pepper.

He opens it out. We see it's 'Socialist Worker'.

Black writting.

He turns over.

Writting. That – seven . . . Seven per cent . . . on the pop – u
– lation . . . ation . . . bin owning . . . Four'n'eighty . . .
eighty–four . . . per cent, on the wealth.

Long pause.

So.

Pause.

93 . . . per cent on the population . . . bin owning . . . 16 per
cent on the wealth. So . . .

He finds a stub of pencil.

100 per cent. On the population . . . owns 100 per cent on
the wealth.

This seems true but not helpful.

So one per cent on the population . . . bin owning . . . seven
bin divided by 84 . . . bin owning four per cent on seven an
. . . eighty-seven an . . . bin owning . . .

Enter OLIVER *as* RALPH *concludes his calculations.*

Hey, nuncle!

OLIVER. Ar, young Ralph?

RALPH. I bin read here, nuncle –

OLIVER. Ar?

RALPH. As seven'n'eighty per cent on the wealth bin owns four
per cent on the people.

OLIVER. I bin squeezing me adder, young Ralph.

RALPH. An' I allus read here, nuncle –

OLIVER. Ar?

RALPH. As how there'n be a fundamental contradiction atween
the social mode on production an' the private nature on the
ownership on capital.

OLIVER. I bin gang t'chump me tiffin, Ralph.

RALPH. An' I allus read here, nuncle –

OLIVER. Ar?

RALPH. As how no ruling class will bin ever giving up its power winout there be a struggle, creating the need on the armed struggle for us to be wresting it of them.

OLIVER. That bin sounding to me as stippling talk, young Ralph.

RALPH. An I allus bin read here, nuncle –

A sudden thought.

I'm gang t'tell him.

OLIVER. Telloo?

RALPH. Gang tell Mad Malcolm, Bane on Froth, an all his merrie companye, as how all history bint history on struggle on the common folk for justice, freedom an the seizure on state power.

OLIVER. Ralph –

RALPH. Ar, 'n more, as tis only the common folk can bin fulfilling the historic role win providing the agency on revolutionary change.

OLIVER. Ralph –

RALPH. Ar, 'n more, agin, as on the need to build a revolutionary vanguard in the working class, for as how an there'n none, the working class falls prey to false counsel, fallolloping and revisionism.

RALPH *striding out.*

OLIVER. Ralph son on Rolf what bin it as you'm doing –

RALPH. I bin telling 'em!

He flings the flag into a bush and strides out. A third grouse flies out. OLIVER watches, horrified. From the other side of the stage, a shout. It is the BANE, who, it should be noted, speaks a strange and confusing language, a translation of which is appended.

BANE *(off).* Tear! (*THERE.*)

RALPH *(off).* Hey! Youn! Mad Malcolm Bane on Froth!

BANE *(off).* Snare! (*THERE.*)

RALPH *(off).* Hey! Youn!

BANE *(off).* Spare! (*THERE.*)

Two shots. RALPH *staggers on clutching a grouse and his stomach.*
He falls, dying.

OLIVER (*rushes to* RALPH). O Ralph son on Rolf. O Ralph son
on Rolf as me'n me dam took in when yourn blain died. O
Ralph son on Rolf as I swore at yourn blain as I'd keep from
harm an' rollocking. O Ralph son on Rolf –

RALPH. O bugger.

He dies. A HUGE DOG *rollocks on to the stage and finds the grouse.*
A bush slides on. OLIVER *bemused. The* BANE *stands up in the*
bush. He has a gun and a glass of sherry, wears a kilt, carpet slippers
and talks in an upper-class English accent.

BANE (*as the* DOG *bounds over to him*). Hell one, Grover, hell one.
(*WELL DONE, ROVER, WELL DONE.*) (*He takes the grouse from*
the DOG. OLIVER *looking at the bush. To explain.*) His eyes.
Toe-while nut. Loo a heater? (*DISGUISE. MOBILE BUTT. YOU*
A BEATER?)

OLIVER. Ar.

BANE. Sell fun, Plover. Might. Sets woe. (*WELL DONE, ROVER.*
RIGHT. LET'S GO.) (*Notices body.*) Sky Shod. (*MY GOD.*)
(*To* OLIVER.) Why spleen, tots cat? Cry odd. (*I MEAN,*
WHAT'S THAT? MY GOD.)

OLIVER. I'm sorry, sir.

BANE. Why nod. (*MY GOD.*)

OLIVER. I'm sorry, sir.

BANE. Buy cod. (*MY GOD.*)

OLIVER. I'm sorry, sir, for spoiling yourn shoot, sir.

BANE. Wry bod. (*MY GOD.*)

OLIVER. I'm sorry, sir, for spoiling yourn shoot with this here
shameful incident, sir.

BANE. Try Tod. (*MY GOD.*)

OLIVER. An' I'm right sorry, sir, for really buggering up yourn
monning an the monning on the fine ladies an gennlemen
on yourn companye, sir. (*Afterthought.*) An he'm right sorry
too.

BANE. Wits call bright, bold roy. Tits ball shite. Fly sod. Over.
(*ITS ALL RIGHT, OLD BOY, IT'S ALL RIGHT. MY GOD.
ROVER.*)

The BANE *gets in his bush and exits. The* DOG *follows.*

OLIVER. O Ralph son on Rolf. Learn youn ne'er. Things is as
ought to be. What is, ist as it should. Bin youn still living,
allus say never. What seem certain be certain. Never bint
gang t'come. All else be chaos, darkness and confusion.

Lights fade to blackout.

Scene Three

Lights discover a SPECTATOR *at a cricket match. In front of his seat is a
white line, the boundary, and in front of that stands* JACK, *a fielder. The*
SPECTATOR *is in shirt sleeves. He has a pocket chess set. It's a hot, lazy
day. The sound of the match, three balls, ending the over, and smatterings of
applause. At each ball* JACK *tenses, then relaxes. At the end of the over, he
turns to the* SPECTATOR, *who shows him the chessboard.*

JACK. Knight to Queen's Rook four.

SPECTATOR. Right.

The SPECTATOR *makes the move as* JACK *exits. A moment or two,
then enter* RON, *another fielder. He smiles at the* SPECTATOR,
who smiles back. Sound of the first ball of the new over. Then.

SPECTATOR. He's threatening your bishop.

RON. Eh? Is he?

SPECTATOR (*showing him the board*). Mm.

RON. Oh, damn. I thought he might do that.

SPECTATOR. What you going to do?

RON. I think – a little muse.

Sound of ball. Offhand, in direction of field.

Well played.

Applause.

I think – pawn to King Three.

SPECTATOR *shrugs, makes the move.*

Not bad, is he?

SPECTATOR. No.

Ball. Applause.

RON. What's that for? Only a single.

SPECTATOR. Fifty partnership. Only the third this season.
Between numbers eight and eleven. In under 90 minutes.
One of them left-handed. On a Friday.

RON. Ah.

Pause.

Let me look at that again.

SPECTATOR *shows* RON *the board.*

No, no way out. Damn clever.

SPECTATOR. Mm.

Pause. Ball.

RON. What's he like?

SPECTATOR. Who?

RON (*gestures to board*). Him. Jack.

SPECTATOR. Oh, he's – don't you know him?

RON. No, we've never met.

SPECTATOR. But –

RON. Other side of the park, you see. Always, the opposite side.

SPECTATOR. I don't know him well.

RON. Good to find out, what he's like. What makes him tick. His
thoughts, on things. You know?

SPECTATOR. Mm. Well, I could ask him, if you like.

RON. Yes. Thanks. Yes, I'd like that very much.

SPECTATOR. Right, then.

Sudden ball. Applause.

Lord, that was quick.

RON (*vaguely*). Wasn't it.

SPECTATOR. Bouncer.

RON. Yes. He doesn't seem too happy.

SPECTATOR. Who?

RON. The bowler. Shouting, something. Quite upset. I can't see
why. The batsman seemed to hit the thing all right.

SPECTATOR. I think that's why –

RON. Oh, yes.

Slight pause.

They do, don't they, shout a lot. And drink. An awful lot.
Lager. From cans. Ice-cold. You know?

SPECTATOR. You don't approve?

Ball.

RON. Well, only insofar, the English youngsters . . . lose their
chance, you know, if all the time we're hiring . . . Not that I
object on grounds of *that*, you know, I mean, I've no
objections on the grounds of *that* at all.

SPECTATOR. You'd let your daughter marry one?

RON. Australian? Not sure I'd go that far. Would you?

SPECTATOR *smiles*.

Ah. Over.

Exit RON. *Pause. Enter* JACK.

JACK. What's he done?

SPECTATOR. You've got his bishop.

JACK (*looks at board, moves*). Great. Great. And well set up. No
bother.

Ball.

SPECTATOR. You'll have to be quick. It's a quarter to six. Their
last man in.

JACK. And a bumping pitch and a blinding light and an hour to play and they're in the shite.

SPECTATOR. What?

JACK. Henry Newbolt. Sir Henry, I should say. You know, that ghastly poem. Breathless hush. Play up and play the sodding game. Shoved down our throats at school.

SPECTATOR. Oh, yes.

Ball.

VOICE. OW!

JACK (*pleased*). See that? Right between the legs. You could hear the crack of ball on box from here. That's what I like. Attacking play.

SPECTATOR. Mm. Controversial.

JACK. Well, different attitude. Our commonwealth cousins. I mean, they learn it in the jungle. Shinning coconuts at monkeys. Kill or be killed, out there. The tribal ritual.

SPECTATOR. I'm not so sure there's that much jungle left in Kingston.

JACK. Way they think. I like it. Spunk.

SPECTATOR. Batsman still hopping round.

JACK. He's playing up.

SPECTATOR. I wouldn't like to face him.

JACK. Nor would we. That's why we bought him.

Ball.

SPECTATOR. He asked what you were like.

JACK. Who?

SPECTATOR. Ron.

JACK. Oh, Ron. Yes. Odd, we've never met. So what d'you say?

SPECTATOR. I said I didn't know.

Pause.

I said I'd ask you. How you tick. Your attitudes, to things.

JACK. Not easy.

Ball.

SPECTATOR. Politics?

JACK. Oh, Tory.

SPECTATOR. Hanging.

JACK. Far too good for 'em.

SPECTATOR. The immigrants.

JACK. I'd send 'em back. Except for him, of course.

SPECTATOR. The place of women.

JACK. Prone.

SPECTATOR. And sportsmanship?

JACK. I never touch it. What?

Ball.

SPECTATOR. It matters not who's won or lost, but how you play the game?

JACK. Ridiculous. Of course it bloody matters.

SPECTATOR. Right. I'll tell him.

JACK. Good.

Ball. He makes to go. Afterthought.

Oh, by the way, find out what he's like, would you?

SPECTATOR. Yes, I will.

Exit JACK. Pause. Enter RON.

RON. What's he done?

SPECTATOR. He's bagged your bishop.

RON. Yes. I s'pose he would. I think I'll have to have another little muse.

Ball. Applause.

What's that for?

SPECTATOR. First time a blue-eyed Lancastrian Number Eleven playing for a southern county in a Gallagher and Lyle three day's scored more than sixteen in two overs facing right-hand bowling from a four-times warned Australian.

RON. I see.

Long pause. Ball.

It's getting quite exciting, isn't it?

SPECTATOR. Yes.

RON. What do they need?

SPECTATOR. Twelve. And two overs after this to do it.

RON. Breathless hush.

SPECTATOR. You what?

RON. 'There's a breathless hush in the Close tonight,
An hour to play and a match to win,
A bumping pitch and a blinding light,
An hour to play and the last man in.
And it's not for the sake of a ribboned coat,
Or the selfish hope of a season's fame:
But his Captain's hand on his shoulder smote:
"Play up! play up! and play the game" '.

Sir Henry Newbolt. Poem. Made to learn it as school. And jolly glad I was.

SPECTATOR. Yes.

Ball.

RON. Did you find anything out, about him?

SPECTATOR. Yes. He knows the poem, too.

RON. Splendid.

SPECTATOR. He asked about you.

RON. What did you say?

Ball.

SPECTATOR. I said I didn't know. Your attitudes. To politics, say.

RON. Oh, I'm a bit of a soggy liberal, I'm afraid.

SPECTATOR. To hanging.

RON. Sorry, don't like it, to be frank.

SPECTATOR. The immigrants.

RON. Oh, tolerance and mutual respect.

SPECTATOR. To him?

RON. Well, tolerance.

SPECTATOR. The place of women?

RON. Same again.

SPECTATOR. And sportsmanship?

RON. You know, it's my belief, it matters not who's won or lost, but how you played the game.

Ball.

So what's he like.

SPECTATOR (*suddenly*). Oh, look at that.

RON. At what?

SPECTATOR. Just that.

RON (*confused*). Oh, yes . . .

Looks at board.

I'll move my king. Queen's bishop one.

Ball.

VOICE. OW!

A horrid Australian cackle.

RON. I wish he wouldn't be so . . . noisy.

Exit RON. Pause. Enter JACK.

JACK. What's he done?

SPECTATOR *shows him the board.*

The silly twit.

He moves.

SPECTATOR. But nice.

Ball.

JACK. What's nice?

SPECTATOR. He is. Nice man.

JACK. Like me?

SPECTATOR. We did agree – you shared, um – Look at that.

JACK. At what? There's nothing happening.

SPECTATOR. That's true.

JACK. Now, you were saying?

Ball. Applause.

Bloody hell. You know, these sods might even do it.

SPECTATOR. One over, after this. Need eight. Last man.

JACK. Yes. Yes. They've not a cat in hell's.

Ball.

VOICE. OW!

JACK. Specially with Sambo and his short-pitched risings, eh?

SPECTATOR. State of the nation?

JACK. Beg your pardon?

SPECTATOR. I just wondered what you thought. The state of
England.

JACK. England, eh?

SPECTATOR. That's right.

Pause.

JACK. Think – seedy, threadbare. Now. That's what I think of
England.

SPECTATOR. I see.

Ball. Applause.

Neat single.

JACK. Quite unloveable. I think: of England.

SPECTATOR. Right.

JACK. Just all around, decay.

SPECTATOR. I'll tell him.

Ball. Applause.

And another. Five to draw, and six to win.

JACK. A land obsessed with being second-rate. I mean, why aren't they honest, make Jack Jones Prime Minister? A land without a will. I mean, it's high time Profit ceased to be a dirty word. A land without a backbone. Well, I mean, we're always hearing all about South Africa, but what about what's happening in Russia? Land of the invertebrates. That's what I think, of England.

SPECTATOR. Right.

Ball. Applause.

A two. Just need the four to win. One over, left.

JACK. England, a land: Diseased.

Exit JACK. *Pause. Enter* RON.

SPECTATOR. He's threatening your castle now.

RON (*looking at board, then moving*). Oh, good lord. Um – there. Though I'm not sure that doesn't put me in a Queen-vulnerable situation.

Ball. Applause.

SPECTATOR. They'll never get it, now. With Bruce. Bouncers, the last two, bound to be.

Pause.

RON. What did he say?

SPECTATOR. He wondered what you thought of England.

Ball.

RON. England.

SPECTATOR. Yes.

RON. I'm fond of England.

SPECTATOR. Yes?

RON. I'm very fond.

Ball.

SPECTATOR. Now? Like it, now?

RON. Yes, yes. Think, now, more than ever, actually.

    Ball.

VOICE. OW! CHRIST!

    Horrid Australian cackle.

SPECTATOR. Two left.

RON. Oh yes, I wish he wouldn't –

    Ball.

VOICE. OW!

SPECTATOR. You don't feel . . . seedy?

RON. England? No, it's gentle.

SPECTATOR. Threadbare? Inefficient?

RON. Tenderly.

SPECTATOR. Invertebrate?

RON. Perhaps, but loveable.

SPECTATOR (*stands*). One ball, one ball – to do it all . . .

    Ball. And it comes, high, towards RON, *who leaps, misses, crashes to the ground.*

RON. Oh blu – bu – bother.

    JACK *runs in, in some passion. He looks down at* RON, *who looks up. Pause.*

RON (*in great pain, extends his hand*). How – do – you – do – Jack. And do please call me Ron.

JACK. You silly bastard.

RON. What?

JACK. You stupid fucker. Missing that.

RON. I tried.

JACK. We would have won.

RON. I did my best.

JACK. Your best was not sufficient. Silly fucker.

SPECTATOR *proffers the board to* JACK, *who moves*.

King takes castle.

SPECTATOR. Mate.

RON. I tried. I tried.

Blackout. Then, at once, spot on SPECTATOR. *Music builds up during.*

SPECTATOR. The sand on the desert is sodden red,
    Red with the wreck of a square that broke;
    The gatling's jammed and the Colonel dead,
    And the Regiment blind with the dust and smoke.
    The river of death has brimmed its banks,
    And England's far and honour's a name,
    But the voice of a schoolboy rallies the ranks:
    'Play up! play up! and play the game!'

Blackout.

Scene Four

In the darkness, a fanfare. Then a spot on a SHOT-PUTTER. *He wears a track suit, stands in a white circle, in a hero's pose. Hold. Then a gunshot.* PUTTER *jumps and general lights up. The* PUTTER *looks, angrily, to the source of the shot, which is a* COMMENTATOR, *with a starting pistol and a microphone. The* COMMENTATOR *is speaking silently into his microphone, and watching an offstage* RUNNER *run round from the back of the audience. The* PUTTER *joins the eye-follow of the* RUNNER. *From the shot to the appearance of the* RUNNER, *about half a minute. The* RUNNER *runs across the stage, and we hear, while we see him, the* COMMENTATOR'*s words. The* RUNNER *is in vision for five seconds, as he will be on each entrance through the scene.*

COMMENTATOR. And already after only half a lap he's way out
    in front and

And the COMMENTATOR *back to silent commentary. The* PUTTER *glares after the* RUNNER, *for five seconds, during which he consults a stopwatch. Then he picks up a shot, puts it to his neck, feels the weight. Takes the shot down, rubs it. All this takes 20 seconds. He looks at us and speaks.*

PUTTER. The Olympic Movement. The ideal. That from all lands, and from all walks of life, young men and women, best of their breed, shall come together, to compete. No, not to win. Working to win. Straining and sweating in the hope of winning. But, ultimately, not to win. But to have taken part.

Pause.

A contradiction. And a paradox. It matters not, who's won or lost. A contradiction. For it matters mightily.

RUNNER *runs across, the same direction as before. Again, we hear the* COMMENTATOR*'s words while the* RUNNER*'s in vision.*

COMMENTATOR. The end of one and a half laps eleven laps to go one minute thirty-seven seconds

PUTTER *glowers after the* RUNNER *for five seconds, consulting his stopwatch. Then he speaks.*

PUTTER. Born in a northern town. Big, even then. My mother knew, been in a fight when she had me. It started at the breast, I think. Was sucking mother's milk. Then suddenly, by accident, it fell. Big breast, my mum. Big, round, and heavy. Pendulous. Fell on my little neck. My little pudgy hand, reached up, to push it. Felt it, there. Against my neck. And pushed. Into her flesh. Then, knew. Then, realized. Vocation. I had found, then, what I wanted most to do.

RUNNER *crosses the stage.*

COMMENTATOR. Beginning to stretch out now as with this punishing pace . . .

PUTTER *looks after the* RUNNER, *three seconds, stopwatch. He prepares to take a put as he speaks.*

PUTTER. The practice. First, the stance. The body weight on right leg. The right foot placed along the diameter of the circle. Left leg, knee bent, touching the ground with tiptoes. Trunk, upright. The left arm raised. The bend. Trunk forward. Left leg raised. Left arm hangs. The left leg in, towards the right. The swing. Extend the left leg. Flight. Hop once, right foot to the centre, left still straight. Transfer. The shift. The shoulder raised, the knee is straightened. The right arm thrusts and –

He's about to put when he's interrupted by the COMMENTATOR *and the* RUNNER*'s cross.*

COMMENTATOR. and still with the gap widening it's 65 a lap and how long can he –

PUTTER *looks after* RUNNER *for three seconds. Stopwatch. He sits at the beginning of this speech.*

PUTTER. Started throwing at the age of 18 months. A great big blob of baby's egg and bacon breakfast, from the carry-cot position. With a coronation spoon. First tries, a failure. No throws. Then, I hit a plaster duck. Six feet. Not bad, a nipper, eh? Moved on. The age of two. A plate. Eight feet. And thought of changing to the discus. No. No. Cricket ball. By this time, three. Nine feet. Technique developing. Got granma right between the eyes.

RUNNER *crosses stage.*

COMMENTATOR. – and at this pace we're set to equal the world record here

PUTTER *stands, looks after* RUNNER, *stopwatch. Five seconds. Prepares to put during this speech.*

PUTTER. The principle. All body forces, all available, combine, contributing to the throw. Exerted, forces, in the proper order, timed each to build on what has gone before. The horizontal force becomes the vertical. The greater force exerted on the ground, the greater speed, the object, in the air. The higher angle, further throw, up to the optimum, 42 degrees. So angle, force, combine. But not brute force. Scientific, pure. All angled to one moment, of release. Force, but not brute. Not aftershave made flesh. But –

He's about to put as RUNNER's *entrance interrupts.*

COMMENTATOR. But with early six minutes gone and seven laps to go and it still looks like

PUTTER *looks after* RUNNER, *three seconds, stopwatch. Sits for the speech.*

PUTTER. Went to a grammar school. You see, not dumb. Not brute. But laughed at. Funny voice. Hands like hams. Embarrassed to put up, in class. For quite a time, I wondered. But then, resolve. A choice – it must be made. For a shot-putter must eat. Eat hugely. Half pound steaks for breakfast. 20 eggs a day. In his dotage, muscles underused, grows gross and flabby. But a sacrifice worth making. As

Achilles made the choice between a short and glorious life, or lengthy mediocrity. And I chose glory, and my arms are rigid with best fillet, hooped with rump and porterhouse.

RUNNER *crosses the stage.*

COMMENTATOR. upped his pace to 60 seconds and it seems he's set to equal the world

PUTTER *stands, three seconds, stopwatch. During this speech, he prepares to put.*

PUTTER. Now. Jumping. Well, all right. For some. But too much going on. Too many factors. Not scientific. Neither pure. Run-up. Take-off. Landing. Could break the record in the air, but get a red, take off before the board. Not pure physique, you see. Untidy. Long jump. High jump. And the polevault. Well. What kind of event's that? You've got an aid. The bleeding pole. Does the job for you, bending back, all that vibrant fibreglass. So where's the skill in that? Might as well take the lift. That's what I say. But then –

He's interrupted by the RUNNER's *cross.*

COMMENTATOR. Then, and yes he's kept it up another minute lap eight minutes gone five laps to –

PUTTER *looks after* RUNNER, *stopwatch, five seconds. This speech again preparing to put.*

PUTTER. And running. Well. I mean. With jumping, least you got some kind of unity, some kind of purpose, that's defined, to counteract the laws of Isaac Newton, for a moment, break the chains of nature, fly. Yur. But running. What a mess. You start, point A. Propel yourself. Spiking the opposition, psychologically. Point B. Point C. Point D. And back again. Point A. Back where you started. All them tactics. Back, square one. And, for that, they cheer you, worship you, and hang your neck about with gold and silver. Well, I ask you. Where's the point in that.

He's about to put as the RUNNER *crosses.*

COMMENTATOR. That's down to one minute ten, conserving strength with just four laps to go and now he's

PUTTER *looks, stopwatch, three seconds. He prepares to put.*

PUTTER. So there it is. You takes your choice. Which, which of them may be described, the summit of the physical accomplishments. I know my choice. That moment, one, split-second moment, when each limb, each muscle, every quivering tendon's set to one objective, one sublime achievement, at the instant of release. United. In that instant. All man's strength, and yes, too, all his delicacy. Balance. Form. Like crystals. Perfect form. It's not a sport. It's not a pastime, game. It's bleeding poetry. An image of pure order. Abstract order. At the instant of release. The classical. Apotheosis. And –

Interrupted by RUNNER.

COMMENTATOR. And yes although he's slowed down he's dead on timing target to equal the world record yes he –

PUTTER *stopwatch, two seconds. The speech is out front, angry.*

PUTTER. But it's not seen. Oh, no. Not seen like that. Like seen at school, it is, brute force, that's how it's seen, regarded. All the grammar boys, those of the toffeed noses, oh, they were all runners, tactics, strategy, do down the other bloke, muddying up the purity of form. And still, here, look, look, look at him. All eyes on him. As he runs on. From A to A. All eyes on him. The crowd gone silent. Tension cracks the eardrums, crackles like electricity, as he runs on, to win his gold. Oh, yes. Oh, yes. I'll get my gold. But winning it in secret. Winning it alone. Cos all them, all you, look at him. And no-one looks at me.

RUNNER *crosses.*

COMMENTATOR. One lap to the bell and he's back up to 60 seconds and it looks as if bar a disaster

PUTTER *two seconds, stopwatch. During this speech he prepares for his shot, re-consulting stopwatch.*

PUTTER. And so I thought. Had the idea. See, a putter has ideas. Oh, yes. A beautiful idea. A perfect concept. Calculated to the enth degree. Run through computers, double-checked. To work, a metre makes the difference. One second is eight metres. Heading, he is, to equal the world record. So. On the backstraight. 200 metres from home. 28 seconds from the tape. Then, it is done.

He doesn't look as the RUNNER *crosses and the bell goes.*

COMMENTATOR. The bell it's 56 to go to equal the world
    record set by –

*PUTTER concluding his preparations, and building up to put, during
this speech, lasting 28 seconds.*

PUTTER. And leaves the arm, correct, at 42 degrees. The only
    thing, it's in the wrong direction. Not in, towards the field,
    but out, towards the track. 18 metres. Easy. At the point of
    shot, a brainstorm. Nothing I could do. Career is ended, yes,
    but what a way to go. A sacrifice. A holy, Grecian sacrifice.
    Achilles. Heel. Across the circle. Perfect concept. Perfect
    MUR-DER. . . .

He puts, over the heads of the audience, falls, immobile.
*COMMENTATOR looks up, stops his commentary, horrified. Hold
this 20 seconds.*

PUTTER. Done. It.

*Enter the RUNNER, breasts an imaginary tape, slow motion, fist
aloft in triumph, holds.*

What. What. What.

COMMENTATOR *looks at* PUTTER.

Missed. What. What.

COMMENTATOR *goes to* PUTTER.

Perfect. Calculations. Couldn't fail. What. What.

COMMENTATOR. Wrong record.

PUTTER. What.

COMMENTATOR *helps him up, keeps hold of his arm, custodially.*

COMMENTATOR. World record. It was broken. Last weekend,
    in Zurich. Or in Oslo. Or at Crystal Palace. One of them.
    With a full house and a Sri Lankan pacemaker. Knocked a
    full point seven of a second off.

PUTTER. What. What.

COMMENTATOR *(leading him out)*. Or, put another way, old
    chum, you're just point seven of a second, just five metres
    sixty centimetres, out of step with history.

They are gone as the RUNNER leaps into the air.

RUNNER. GERONIMO!

Blackout.

Scene Five

In the darkness, at once, the thump of a heart and the faint drumming of hooves and a breathless taped VOICE.

VOICE. Here we go. Coming up to First Bank. Nice and quiet. Eight strides. Five, three and o–oo–oo–over –

THUMP thump thump thump thump.

No trouble. Now just keep our cool. Round we go. That's it. Concentrate. One at a time. What's next. Irish Bank. Gorblimey. No. OK. And steady as she go–oo–oo–oes –

THUMP thump thump thump thump.

Easy. Easy. Bom bom bom. Easy. Bom bom bom. Right. On we go. Gawd, this place is a mess. Look at that. Champagne corks littering the fairway. Empty tins of pate de campagne disfiguring the greensward. I dunno – Concentrate! Lambert's Sofa, this one can be tricky, five three tw–wow–o–oo–ooo –

THUMP thump thump thump thump.

Not bad. Not too bad. Now. Don't overdo it. Tight at the back. Keep cool. Capability Cutting. Piece of cake. Jump, and think of the Olympics. Three two ga–a–a–aw–awd –

THUMP thump thump thump thump. Lights fading up.

All right. Just. Close. All right. Don't – careful, woman, that's my mouth you're pulling – Gawd, she's going at a lick . . . Now, what's this? The Double Coffin, oh, come on love, let's take the easy way, I mean I know it adds a couple of seconds but for the sake of my peace of mi–i–i–iiind –

THUMP thump thump thump thump.

Close. But over. Right. Ooh, look, isn't that the Royal Range Rover? Concentrate. Keep going. The Trocarno. Gawd, she's pushing it. What does she think I am, a Mazzarati? What's the matter with her? Has she got a dinner da-a-a-aaate - ?

THUMP thump thump thump thump. Lights full.

She's pissed. I swear she's zonked out of her tiny skull. She ought to get run in. She is drunk in charge of a four-footed friend and the F.F.F. in question is - gawd it's the Trout Hatchery - we'll never - not at this pace - we're going to - hold on to your seat mate - what goes up must come dow-ow-oo-ar-aa-aarrghh . . .

Splash and a HORSE *staggers on to the stage. The* HORSE *is two men,* FRONT *and* BACK. FRONT *- who was the* VOICE *- has a wire head and platform hooves.* BACK *holds* FRONT *round the middle and wears platform hooves and a wire tail.* BACK *is hopping on a hurt leg.*

FRONT. I knew it, I knew it -

BACK. Ooh me leg.

FRONT. I knew that third tequila was a mistake, but would she listen?

BACK (*falls*). Oh, blimey -

FRONT (*falls with* BACK). What the hell's up with you?

BACK. Me leg's gorn.

FRONT. You sure?

BACK. Course I'm bleeding sure.

FRONT. Broken?

BACK. In several places, mate.

FRONT. Oh, gawd, she's coming. Get up.

BACK. Get up?

FRONT (*struggling to pull* BACK *up with him*). Pretend you're all right.

BACK. What d'you mean? My leg's gorn. I need treatment.

FRONT. Oh for Gawd's sake -

BACK. I need a stretcher and nice men with hypodermics and an ambulance dash through the night to St Hippolyta's -

FRONT (*pulling*). Come on, brother –

BACK. And all tucked up in a nice warm private stall with clean hay and a crisp starched rug and gentle stable-girls wiping my fevered brow –

FRONT has managed to get BACK *up.*

FRONT. Look, mate, forget your turgid fantasies.Have you any idea what they do to horses with broken legs?

BACK. No, what do they –

WOMAN'S VOICE (*off*). Forelock!

FRONT. Well, in a word –

Enter a young woman RIDER. *She is dripping wet, played by a man, and very cross.*

RIDER. Forelock.

FRONT (*desperately backing round to hide* BACK, *who is valiantly trying to disguise his broken leg*). Oh, 'allo, miss.

RIDER. I mean, fuck it, Forelock.

FRONT. Sorry about that, miss. Bit of a prang.

RIDER. I mean, for fuck's sake.

FRONT. I just lost me balance, miss, it can happen to anyone –

RIDER. I mean of all the fucking, clumsy, clodhopping – I mean, Trout Hatchery's a piece of piss, Forelock, it's easier than shitting in a fucking bucket. I mean, you went over that like a fucking carthorse. What are you, a fucking carthorse? Dobbin? Is that what I'm going to have to shitting call you? Fucking Dobbin?

BACK. Look, do we have to stand here and take this lying down?

FRONT. Just shut up and look guilty.

BACK. Guilty?

FRONT. While she's shouting, she in't shooting.

BACK collapses, bringing FRONT *down with him.*

BACK (*as he goes*). Shoo – oo –

RIDER. Eh?

FRONT. You great idiot!

BACK. Sorry. It was just –

RIDER. Forelock?

FRONT. Look what you done now.

BACK. It was the shock of –

RIDER (*rushing to the* HORSE). Forelock, are you all right?

FRONT. See?

RIDER. Your leg? Forelock? Hurt?

BACK. Hurt, woman, is something of a –

FRONT. That's right, miss, just a slight bruise, minor abrasions, no need to –

RIDER (*kneeling beside the* HORSE). You've broken your leg –

BACK. Yur, I have, and if you'd care to ring for a –

FRONT. Well, just a bit, you know, just a sort of mild multiple fracture, nothing to worry –

RIDER (*holding the* HORSE). Oh, Forelock, it's your *leg* –

BACK. Well, it's not me cock, is it?

RIDER. Oh, Forelock, what am I to do?

FRONT. Just don't do anything rash, that's all –

RIDER. Oh, Forelock, how will you ever forgive me?

BACK. Forgive? What for?

FRONT. I've a horrible feeling we're about to find out.

RIDER (*out front, surprisingly*). And she thought at that moment of the times they'd had together, she, the beautiful, rich, foul-mouthed daughter of the Shadow Leader of the House of Lords, and he, her mount, the beast of burden – oh how 'beast', how 'burden', how the words themselves were paltry, undermined, no, dirtied, made unclean the feelings that she held towards him, her proud beast, and she the all too gross, unworthy burden –

BACK. What's she on about?

FRONT. I neither know, mate, nor wish to discover. Just keep smiling.

BACK. Eh?

RIDER. And of the times they'd spent, travelling together, he in his box and she piloting the landrover, from gymkhana to gymkhana, and of the nights she's been with him in his stable, the mucking out done, and she'd stood there, until the faint sounds of the morning drifted across from the West Wing, and she'd still be there, standing, immobile, drinking in the sight and smell of him, that smell, that wonderful and blissful pungent odour –

BACK. I think she fancies you, mate.

FRONT. Why lay it all on me?

RIDER. And now to be faced with this dilemma – no, more than a dilemma, to be stretched on the rack of his broken body, lying in her arms, the choice that must, at once, be made, no choice, for what was choice? She knew what she must do. But what was know? and what was must? And was must what she knew? Or knowing what she must?

BACK. I'm finding all of this very hard to follow.

RIDER (*drawing out a huge, ugly pistol*). And thought, one thought above all others, that it would be her, she'd do it, though her being, whole, shrank from the thought as, once she'd read, some flowers shrink with all their being from the light . . .

BACK. Uh . . . What's that?

FRONT. What does it look like?

BACK. She's a bleeding psychopath.

FRONT. They're all bleeding psychopaths.

BACK. You don't mean . . . I mean . . . they don't shoot horses, do they?

FRONT. Well, in brief, the answer to that question is –

RIDER. And here she was, looking down into his big brown eyes, moist and yielding, and she held the weapon in her hand and its smooth, sterile, frigid coldness, and the soft warmth of his sweating flank as it breathed beneath her trembling hand . . .

BACK. So what we going to do?

FRONT. We've only one chance, mate. Sometimes they keep 'em, broken leg and all, for stud. Otherwise it's not worth it. So then they . . . But for stud . . . So let's keep calm, I'll look pathetic and you look virile.

BACK. Virile? After that scrape over Capability Cutting it looks like a bleeding pine cone.

FRONT. Well, if not, it's hi-ho Silver, mate. Look, if nothing else, try and shiver a bit. Show her there's life in the old horse –

RIDER. Yet it wasn't just his body, now, but something else, she felt, some undefinable – and yet, she knew, an instant, that he, in that moment, was no longer beast and she no longer burden, both of them had been translated, no, transubstantiated, and his flesh felt light and silky, almost gossamer, not there, he wasn't there, or rather he was everywhere, his quiet vibrations everywhere, a strange and moving sound, ethereal, the music of the spheres –

BACK. Eh?

FRONT. This is way over.

RIDER. No longer beast, no longer animal, but now super-human – suddenly she realised that as the flesh decayed the Horse was no more Horse and she was no more Rider – she was worshipper, the suppliant, the acolyte, and he was – Hippos! Suddenly, aloud, cried: Hippos! Hippos! Hippos!

BACK. Hippos? The name's Forelock.

RIDER. Hippos – in one, last, strangled cry – what was to do had now, must now be done – Hippos! Hippos! Farewell!

An awful pause. The RIDER *aiming, her face frozen in agony.*

FRONT. Mate?

BACK. Yes mate?

FRONT. I think we blew it.

She squeezes the trigger as blackout. Hugely, Mozart's Requiem. Then lights on the winged HORSE *flying through the skies.*

HORSE (*unison*). From the Horses of Diomedes that Heracles did slay

To the mounts of the six hundred that perished in a day
From apocalyptic palfreys winging death, disease and rage
To those who get their eyes put out upon the West End stage
From Red Rum to the primal steeds that galloped round
    Stonehenge
All with a single, strangled neigh, cry out the word:
    REVENGE!

Blackout.

End of Act One.

ACT TWO

Ball Boys

A locker room,. Enter RUPERT *with a chair. He is a small boy, played by an actor, wearing shorts and a two-tone shirt. He looks round, places the chair carefully. Exit. He re-enters with another chair, places it about ten feet from the other chair. He takes a roll of catgut from his pocket and ties a piece between the two chairs. He goes out and re-enters with a tennis ball. He places it on the floor, below the centre of the line. He goes and crouches by one of the chairs. A moment. Then he runs across, still at the crouch, picks up the ball, and to the other chair. We realise he's a ball boy.* RUPERT *sets the ball centre again, and runs across picking it up. He does this a couple of times – once he misses – before* ONEEYE *enters.* ONEEYE *is another, two-eyed, ball boy. He watches* RUPERT. RUPERT *is concentrating too hard to notice* ONEEYE. ONEEYE *sits on one of the chairs and sticks his leg out.* RUPERT *runs past and trips over. Pause.*

RUPERT. Hallo, Oneeye.

ONEEYE. Hallo, Rupert.

> *Pause.*

RUPERT. That was an unfriendly thing to do, Oneeye.

ONEEYE. It was meant to be, Rupert.

> *Pause.*

RUPERT. Why?

ONEEYE. I'm working out my pique, Rupert. Unable to work it out on those who caused it, they being stronger and more powerful than I, I work it out on the only available person who is weaker and less powerful. In this case, you.

RUPERT. Oh. Right.

> *Pause.* RUPERT *stands. He goes to one of the chairs, crouches, runs through, picking up the ball. Replaces the ball. Looks at* ONEEYE, *grins nervously.*

ONEEYE. Oh, by the way, Rupert.

RUPERT. Yes, Oneeye?

ONEEYE. One question I wanted to ask. Been on my mind. Ever since I came in. Employing my thoughts, my face, before I resolved to catharcize my ire on your person. This query. I wished to put.

RUPERT. Yes, Oneeye?

ONEEYE. What the fuck you playing at, old son?

RUPERT. I was. I was practising.

ONEEYE. Practising.

RUPERT. That's right. The net-run.

ONEEYE. The net-run.

RUPERT. That's right.

ONEEYE. Why, Rupert?

> *Pause.* RUPERT *shrugs.* ONEEYE, *pleasantly.*

Why, Rupert. Old chum.

RUPERT (*coyly*). Well, you know . . .

ONEEYE. Yes. I think I do.

> RUPERT *grins sheepishly.*

You were practising because it's getting close.

> RUPERT *grins sheepishly.*

We're into the fourth round.

> RUPERT *grins sheepishly.*

So you are practising. I understand.

RUPERT. That's good, Oneeye.

ONEEYE. So that you, Rupert, can remove a spent half-lob from before the net so fast that blink you'd miss it.

RUPERT. That's right. Oneeye.

ONEEYE. So that you, Rupert, can clear a volley drop-shot from the park before it hits the ground.

RUPERT. I hope so, Oneeye.

ONEEYE. So that when, on Ladies Semi-Final day, as is
traditional, Mr Dan Mascell has a word of praise for all the
sterling labours of the ball boys, there you'll be, in close-up,
grinning vacuously into number three camera, beamed into
seven million homes.

Pause.

RUPERT. You've hit the spot there, Oneeye.

ONEEYE. WHY.

RUPERT. Why what?

ONEEYE. Why do you wish thus to ascend fame's ladder,
Rupert?

RUPERT. Cos it's there, Oneeye?

ONEEYE. Not for your mother, surely. Not so she can sit before
her 19–inch suffused with the miasma of maternal pride.

Pause.

Her having dumped you. At two months. On the Central
Line. Somewhere between Leytonstone and Ongar.

Pause.

Before, so rumour has it, flinging herself amid the gungy
waters of the Serpentine.

Pause.

RUPERT. Can I please carry on now Oneeye?

ONEEYE. If you like. You've no chance, anyway.

RUPERT. Why not?

ONEEYE. Cos we all know who it will be.

RUPERT. We do?

ONEEYE. It will be he. The boy most likely to. The most
handsome, and most charming, and most cute of all the ball
boys. Nicky Nightlight it will be, in tight-shot, looking as if
he's got half a pound of solid Lurpak in his cheek. He. He.
He. Not you.

Pause.

RUPERT. Why the aggro, Oneeye?

ONEEYE. I AM PIQUED RUPERT.

Pause.

RUPERT. Why?

ONEEYE. Didn't I tell you?

RUPERT. No.

ONEEYE. I got sent off.

Pause.

RUPERT. You can't get sent off, Oneeye. For one, people don't get sent off in tennis, and, for two, you're a ball boy.

ONEEYE. Then I've set a precedent. For off is the direction in which, quite incontravertibly, I was sent.

Pause.

RUPERT. Why?

ONEEYE. Right.

He picks up the ball on the floor, takes another from his pocket, hands both to RUPERT.

You are me. This chair –

He moves one of the chairs to the centre.

Is the centre-line judge. This chair –

He indicates the other chair.

Is the Kerrygold-chewing Nicholas Nightlight. And I – am Sven Svensson, the flying Finn, the blond bombshell, he of the swingeing service and the vicious forehand volley-drop, I am he. OK?

RUPERT. OK.

ONEEYE. Picture the scene. I – that's you – have not had a good day. For a start, on Court No. Two, I was positioned behind old Farty Frobisher, the incontinent net-cord judge, the worst position in all of Surrey, on a hot day, humid, thunderous, knelt right behind that powerhouse of wind. And so, not good. My temper not improved by Madcap Mustovna, the bomber of Bulgaria, who having beat some poor sad sod, in straight sets, flings wide his racket, gesturing his victory,

thrilling the crowd and catching me a nasty blow on the right
temple. With his Latin gesture. In round four. I ask you. So.
Not good. And then, on Court No. One, my woes going up
in the world, the umpire issues his umperial command.

RUPERT. New balls please boys.

ONEEYE. The same. So off we scurry, touching our forelocks,
plunging our puddies into the refridgerated container, that to
preserve the bounce, risking frostbite, tingling the fingers, all
keen and my case despite my throbbing temple and what
then?

RUPERT. What then?

ONEEYE. Hurry up now boys he says.

RUPERT. They always say that. If they're in shot. Always –

ONEEYE. NOT AT ME THEY DON'T.

RUPERT. No, not at you.

Pause.

That's why you got sent off, then, Oneeye?

ONEEYE. No, that is the preamble. This that follows is the
action. You are me. That is Nick Nightlight. I the sainted
Sven. My coming. Paint the scene in words.

Exit ONEEYE.

RUPERT. The Centre Court.
The crowd is hushed.
From face to face we pan. From dowager to dolly, matron to
maiden, virago to virgin. Clutching their tea, unsipped, their
strawberries untasted. All of them, waiting. Looking. Sharp
with expectation.
All's prepared.
The seat umperial. Well stocked. The paper cups are
counted, and the lemon barley water's chilled.
The net, the peace-line, at its centre, hung precisely, to a
millimetre. The ambulances ready. O, St John, thou shouldst
be living at this hour. The barbed wire, slung around the
gleaming greensward.
Groundsmen, in their helmets, with their perspex shields,
run nervous fingers up and down their truncheons. Savage
hounds perambulate.

And, then.
Who knows, who first, the whisper. 'He's coming.' Whispers.
'O, he's coming. Coming. Coming.' Grows to a chant. He's
coming. Coming. Coming. First, but the young, the pre-
pubescent. Then the older join. Spring to November. O he's
coming. Coming. Coming.
Sound like rushing water, or the music of the spheres.
One young Bacchante faints. Another screams. The
groundsmen flex. He's coming. Coming. Coming. Then, he
comes.

Enter ONEEYE *with a racket.*

Stands. Holds up his racket, as if for blessing. For a moment,
but a moment that's eternal, he stands, and nothing moves.
  And then the charge. Wild, screaming, like the horses of
Diomedes that fed on human flesh, first, young and luscious
virgins break across the wire, in platform heels, their imprint
on the sacred turf, then others through the riot lines, young
mothers, screaming, sturdy matrons, then the groupie
grannies too, rush like Niagara across the turf, the sacred
turf, torn flesh, blood on the sacred turf, now two millennia
of civilisation, culminating, as it does, in individual combat
on a Surrey afternoon, upended, wracked, by this outpouring
of a primal energy, from the dark places, from the darkest
depths, a passion uncontrolled, that men have lost the word
for, for the word is worship . . . Then, destroyed. Heads
beaten. Broken souls. The bodies cleared. The acolytes
pressed back. The turf is naked. Once again. A whimper.
Silence. Mystery. The sacrifice is over. The God has spoken.
Being, and becoming, one, that moment. Sven is now the
Universe. The Universe is Sven.

Pause.

ONEEYE. Right. I'm Sven, that's Nicholas, and you're me.

He gives RUPERT *two balls.*

My service.

Serves, with imaginary ball. Ventriloquises.

Out.

He serves again.

An ace. On second serve. 15 love.

He turns to RUPERT, *who is waiting to throw him a ball.* RUPERT *is just about to throw, when* ONEEYE *turns to the chair representing Nick Nightlight, and, in mime, accepts an imaginary ball from him. Serves. Ventriloquises.*

Net!

Different voice:

First service.

Serves again. Takes the return.

A half-lob kills the return. It's 30 love.

The same routine, turning to RUPERT, *who's about to throw, when* ONEEYE *turns away, accepting the ball from the other ball boy.* RUPERT *getting tetchy.* ONEEYE *serves, then misses the return.*

I give away a point. For charity. 30, 15.

He serves with his other ball. Ventriloquises.

OUT!

Same routine. RUPERT *getting very tetchy.*

Ace. 40, 15.

Same routine with RUPERT, *but this time, he leaves it long enough for* RUPERT *to throw the ball.* ONEEYE *has turned, takes a ball from the imaginary ball boy, turns back, sees the ball on the ground in front of him.*

UND VORT IST DA?

RUPERT. My God.

ONEEYE. He says. Und vort ist da.

RUPERT. My Christ.

ONEEYE. He says. To me. Und vort, boya, vort ist da?

RUPERT. My – mother.

ONEEYE. Da? Unt dur grounda, sucred turfa, da?

Pause.

RUPERT. What you do Oneeye.

ONEEYE. We swap.

They swap places. ONEEYE *giving* RUPERT *the racket.*

Go on. Again.

RUPERT (*nervously*). And – wart – is – dar?

> ONEEYE *to* RUPERT, *takes his racket, holds it up, to the crowd, and breaks it across his knee. Presenting the pieces back to* RUPERT.

ONEEYE. Da.

RUPERT. O my God.

ONEEYE (*quickly, out front*). Sven Svensson. Superstar. His habits. Superstitions. Like the taking of one racket, one alone, on to the court.

RUPERT. O my Christ.

ONEEYE. As in the famous final, U.S. Open, he won the fifth set, 27–25, with just four strings intact. The habits, superstititions, of Sven Svensson.

RUPERT. O my – mother.

ONEEYE. So I got sent off.

> *He sits, takes off his shoes and socks, twiddles his toes, during.*

RUPERT. I can understand your pique, now. Crystal clear, your ire now is.

ONEEYE. That's good.

RUPERT. Even the taking out of it on me. Quite comprehensible.

ONEEYE. That's fine.

RUPERT. Unable, as you said, to visit your displeasure on the guilty, you being so much smaller, weaker, yes. Quite clear, that is.

ONEEYE. That's great.

RUPERT. Unwilling to make the leap, from individual oppression to collective strength, unable to build links, between your suffering and the suffering of others, forge a chain that's stronger than its individual parts, unhappy with the old things but unaware of the possibility of change, you find a bogeyman, a scapegoat, any but the real source of exploitation, on to whose shoulders you lay all your pain. I understand.

ONEEYE. You what?

RUPERT. I understand.

ONEEYE. What are you talking about?

Pause.

RUPERT. Been reading.

ONEEYE. What?

RUPERT. Marx. The theses on Feuerbach.

ONEEYE. You who?

RUPERT. Ludwig.

ONEEYE. Beethoven.

RUPERT. No, Feuerbach.

ONEEYE. I see.

RUPERT. The argument of Marx, in his Theses on Feuerbach, this Ludwig Feuerbach, published in 1845, a classic text though not in any sense traditional, his argument is this – that the chief defect of all hitherto existing materialism is that the thing, reality, is conceived only in the form of the object, or of contemplation, but not as human sensuous activity, practice, not subjectively. Or so he says.

ONEEYE. Go on, Rupert.

RUPERT. The dispute, Marx takes the view, over the reality or non-reality of thinking which is isolated from practice is a purely scholastic question.

ONEEYE. Continue, Rupert.

RUPERT. The materialistic doctrine, he continues, that men are products of circumstances and upbringing, and that, therefore, changed men are products of changed upbringing, forgets that it is men that change circumstances and that the educator himself needs educating.

ONEEYE. I think I begin to get your drift, Rupert.

RUPERT. Social life is practical, he says. All mysteries which mislead theory to mysticism find their rational solution in human practice and in the comprehension of this practice.

ONEYE. So?

RUPERT. The philosophers have only interpreted the world, thus does the sage conclude: the point, however, is to change it.

Pause.

ONEEYE. How?

Pause.

RUPERT. He doesn't say.

ONEEYE. Oh?

RUPERT. No.

ONEEYE. He doesn't say.

Pause.

Sven will be still out there, Rupert. His famous grip, on which chapters have been written and from which Mr Mascell gets a delicate frisson of delight, that grip performing yet another function, that of keeping his racket in one piece. Holding together that which is broken. Disguising contradiction. Papering the cracks.

Pause.

He doesn't say.

RUPERT. Perhaps he does later. Other works. I haven't read.

ONEEYE. Perhaps he does.

Pause.

Why's your name Rupert?

RUPERT. Given me.

ONEEYE. Of course. But with what reasoning.

RUPERT (*sits. Enthusiastically*). Well, I suppose, fashions. Reflected perhaps particularly, in naming orphans. Need to integrate them with the fashionable modes. To give them names to, mark their place. To follow trends. But certain trends. Trends of the ruling class. Not Putney names. Not names of the produce of a Chelsea bijou residence. Not Jude or Jason, Damion or Saul. Nor yet the firm and gritty names, the monosyllables, that grace the offspring of the West: the

peasant-dressed, and civil-liberties-obsessed, of Holland Park
or Ladbroke Grove or Hammersmith, their names to conjure
with, like Ned or Sam or Dan or Hank or Ben. Nor yet
provincial names; good, north of Watford names; sound,
honest, *Daily Mail* type names, like Simon, Robin, Timothy or
John. Nor yet West Country names, earth-friendly names,
names of the issue of North Devon commune-makers, ethnic
names, like Gethan, Jethro, Pedr, Rhys or Seth.

Slight pause.

But upper order names. Names of the living dead. Names of
the half-light, those who have outlived their usefulness but
not their power, those who walk in limbo, with death's
fingers in their hair. Like Charles. And St John. Alexander.
Algernon. And Rupert. Burke's peerage names. Hereditary
names. And orphans' names.

Pause.

ONEEYE. Still there.

RUPERT. Who, there?

ONEEYE. Sven. Still out there.

RUPERT. S'pose so.

ONEEYE. Know so. Winning.

Pause.

RUPERT. Why you called Oneeye, Oneeye?

ONEEYE. Didn't I ever tell you?

RUPERT. No.

ONEEYE. Do you know of the Weathermen?

RUPERT. You mean those nice men on the telly with the plastic
charts, then, Oneeye?

ONEEYE. No, Rupert.

RUPERT. Then I don't, no.

Slight pause.

ONEEYE. The Weathermen were an American group of urban
guerrillas who rejected the tactic of peaceful protest on the
one hand, or the forging of links with the proletariat on the

other, and instead resolved to create a revolutionary situation
by individual acts of terror. They, being middle-class and of a
literary bent, decided to choose their name as a reference,
not to they of the isobars and V–shaped depressions over
Iceland, but to a line in a song, the song in question being
Subterranean Homesick Blues by B. Dylan, who had the
advantage of being not only culturally contemporary but also
art. At first they were tempted by the idea of calling
themselves The Vandals, from the line, 'The pump don't
work 'cos the vandals took the handle'. But finally they
settled on The Weathermen, taking their ref. from the line,
'You Don't Need a Weather-Man To Know Which Way The
Wind Blows'. For the irony.

Pause.

RUPERT. Why you called Oneeye, Oneeye?

ONEEYE. The Ballard of a Thin Man. It tells the tale of a man
called Jones, who walks into the room, a pencil in his hand.
At this point, he sees somebody naked, and enquires, who is
that man. He tries so hard, but he can't understand, just
what he will say when he gets home.

RUPERT. Why you called Oneeye, Oneeye?

ONEEYE. A little later this gentleman, this Mr Jones, hands in his
ticket, and goes watch the geek, the precise meaning of which
is obscure. This, geek, in any event, comes up to him, Mr
Jones that is, when he hears him speak, and says, how does it
feel to be such a freak, whereupon he, Mr Jones, says
impossible, as he, the geek, hands him a bone.

RUPERT. Why you called Oneeye, Oneeye?

ONEEYE. The lyric then provides us with some background on
Mr Jones. He's associated with professors, we are told, who
have all liked his books. He's also been involved in medico
criminological research, we gather, for with great lawyers he's
discussed lepers and crooks. But his interests are wider, we
are informed. He is a man with a keen interest in literature.
He's been through, indeed, all Scott Fitzgerald's books, he's
very well read, it's well known.

RUPERT. Why you called Oneeye, Oneeye?

ONEEYE. Back at the plot, a new character, a sword-swallower, comes up to Mr Jones, and, for reasons which are not explained, kneels. He then, for whatever motive, crosses himself, and clicks his high heels. And then without further notice he asks how it feels. And says, in a ghoulish moment, here is your throat back, thanks for the loan.

RUPERT. Why you called Oneeye, Oneeye?

ONEEYE. YOU SEE A ONE-EYED MIDGET SHOUTING THE WORD NOW. AND YOU ASK FOR WHAT REASON AND HE SAYS HOW. AND YOU SAY WHAT DOES THIS MEAN AND HE SCREAMS BACK YOU'RE A COW. GIVE ME SOME MILK OR ELSE GO HOME. AND YOU KNOW SOMETHING IS HAPPENING BUT YOU DON'T KNOW WHAT IT IS DO YOU MR JONES.

Pause.

I do not recall my real name. For I was but a three-month old when my old man and his old dam were gallumphed by a bulldozer while resisting the demolition of their cosy old ancestral family shack.

Slight pause.

Hence my dark thoughts and black imaginings.

Slight pause.

Hence are you with me, Rupert?

RUPERT. With you where, Oneeye?

ONEEYE. Are you going to do it?

RUPERT. Do what?

ONEEYE. What we said.

RUPERT. What you said.

ONEEYE. What I said. You going to do it?

RUPERT. What we –

ONEEYE. Talked about.

RUPERT. I don't –

ONEEYE. Well, Rupert?

RUPERT. Just don't know.

ONEEYE. The point, point being, to change it.

RUPERT. Just don't know.

Pause.

RUPERT. Why – quite the manner – you suggested – quite, such viciousness, quite – such a bloody way.

ONEEYE. I saw IF at an impressionable age.

RUPERT. If?

ONEEYE. Film by Lindsay Anderson. Starring Malcolm MacDowell and Arthur Lowe. Culminated in a machine-gun massacre. The Ultimate Public School Horrorshow. Cornered the market for years. Hundreds of ex-public school writers, wandering round, unable to write the story of their life, forced instead to make agitational propaganda, chock full of unlikely ethnic references, or indulge in obscure fantasies in closed rooms in which the two plumbers who call in Act Two turn out to be the ego and the id.

Pause.

RUPERT. Nick Nightlight went to public school. On a grant. The school had places for orphans, free places, to create a social mix. They're very keen on that, apparently, a social mix. A token prole he was, a token representative of the oppressed orders, an awful reminder of, what's underneath.

Pause.

They treated him just the same, he said. Not toffee-nosed at all. Just because he came from a rotten foster-home, his foster-father beat him up, and his foster-mother beat him up, that didn't stop them treating him just like their mates. And beating him up. With all varieties of weaponry. Just like the others.

Pause.

But forms go deep. Modes, etiquettes and rules, unwritten and unspoken. Nurtured like lawns, through generations. Know every rule, but cannot know the hidden ethos of the British ruling class. Their solidarity. Their law unto themselves.

Pause.

Told, when he arrived, resist all sexual suggestiveness. So, when a pederastic advance was made, resisted. Strongly. Physically.

Pause.

Head of Fives Team. Captain of Rackets. Cock of Squash. His putative seducer.

Pause.

Expelled. Unmiddle-class activities. Poor old Nick.

Pause.

ONEEYE. Well, that's all very interesting, Rupert, but I'm not convinced it's quite germane.

RUPERT. Germane to what?

ONEEYE. The question. Of whether you are going to do it.

Pause.

Let's play a game. While you decide.

RUPERT. What game.

ONEEYE. Suggest.

RUPERT. Manual or intellectual?

ONEEYE. Intellectual.

RUPERT. Darts?

ONEEYE. No, not darts.

RUPERT. Not darts.

ONEEYE. We will play Erudition.

Pause.

RUPERT. Erudition.

ONEEYE. Yes.

To Audience.

Erudition. Pure knowledge. No form, no logical construct, no maths. Just information. Know it or you don't.

RUPERT. I never liked this game.

ONEEYE. Useful for those, as I, whose minds are like the sea, liquid, formless, facts floating like flotsam on the salty brine, unconnected with their purpose or original intent. You start.

RUPERT. Oh, architecture.

ONEEYE. What's a spandrel?

RUPERT. Eh?

ONEEYE. My go. Codenames.

RUPERT. What?

ONEEYE. Codenames of operations. Military operations. As in Overlord.

RUPERT (*shrugs*). Overlord.

ONEEYE. D–Day. Sealion.

RUPERT. Dunkirk?

ONEEYE. Hitler's invasion of Britain.

RUPERT. Didn't happen!

ONEEYE. Had a code. Three. Barbarossa.

RUPERT. Don't know.

ONEEYE. The same's invasion of Russia's stilly wastes. Four. Gemstone.

RUPERT. The bugging of the Watergate Hotel.

ONEEYE. Sod you.

RUPERT. One. My go.

ONEEYE. Come on.

RUPERT. Um, er –

ONEEYE. Come on.

RUPERT. Oh, assemblages.

ONEEYE. Partridges.

RUPERT. A wing? A wing of partridges?

ONEEYE. No, a covey. Five. Tennis.

RUPERT. What?

ONEEYE. Tennis. Ask a question.

RUPERT. Why . . .

ONEEYE. TENNIS.

Pause.

You might ask, who. Did what. To whom. On a sunny. Afternoon. In June.

RUPERT. Don't like this game.

ONEEYE. Darts, then.

RUPERT. You what?

ONEEYE. Darts, then.

RUPERT. But, Oneeye –

ONEEYE (*strides out*). DARTS

Re-enters with six darts.

Bull for start.

He throws, offstage. Pause. RUPERT *throws.*

RUPERT. I think, just slightly nearer, Oneeye.

ONEEYE. Of course you're nearer. You got 25. I missed the board. So – play.

RUPERT. You're sure?

ONEEYE. So PLAY.

RUPERT (*nervously, as he throws*). Missed, Double-20, 20, score 241.

Gets his darts from off, returns, ONEEYE *throws.*

ONEEYE. Single six. Missed the circle. Missed the Board.

RUPERT (*throwing*). Double 20, treble 20, 20, total 121.

ONEEYE (*throwing*). Single ten, single six, missed the circle.

RUPERT (*throwing*). Double 15, eight – losing my touch now, Oneeye –

ONEEYE. Play!

RUPERT (*throws*). Treble 20, score left, 23.

ONEEYE (*throws*). Missed the circle, missed the board, missed the board.

RUPERT. 20. Leaving three.

ONEEYE. One double one.

RUPERT. I never get this –

ONEEYE. Play!

RUPERT (*throws*). One. Double one. I'm sorry, Oneeye, sorry –

ONEEYE. Why?

RUPERT. I won.

ONEEYE. Of course you won!

RUPERT. Perhaps I cheated.

ONEEYE. Hm.

RUPERT. Perhaps you played to lose.

> *Pause.*

You know you're terrible at darts, Oneeye. You're worse at darts than I am at Erudition. Why d'you play it? You never play it. Whenever I suggest it, you get angry. 'Cos you know you'll lose. 'Cos you're so terrible.

ONEEYE. It is not true, Rupert, that the revolutionary, ideally, is the man with nothing to lose. He must have something, two things, still unlost. His anger, and his self-respect. Well?

RUPERT. What?

ONEEYE. Well?

> *Pause. Shouts.*

ONE DOUBLE ONE.

> *Pause.*

RUPERT (*gives up*). I'll do it.

ONEEYE. Why? WHY?

RUPERT. Why?

ONEEYE. Because philosophers have always interpreted the
world, Rupert.

RUPERT. Because philosophers have always interpreted the
world, Oneeye.

ONEEYE. But the point is to change it, Rupert.

RUPERT. But the point is to change it, Oneeye.

ONEEYE. And you are very ugly, Rupert.

RUPERT. And I am very ugly, Oneeye.

In the distance, the sound of screaming girls, coming closer.

ONEEYE. He's coming.

RUPERT. That's Sven?

ONEEYE. Of course it is. Who else?

RUPERT. He's won?

ONEEYE. Of course he has. What else.

RUPERT. So, now?

ONEEYE. Of course, now. When else? You ready?

RUPERT. Yes.

ONEEYE. The catgut, Rupert.

> RUPERT *unties the catgut from the chairs. He stands, holding it.*

> Good.

> *Exit* ONEEYE. *Screaming very close. Slam of a door. Enter* SVEN.
> *He is breathless. He grins at* RUPERT. *Banging on the door and
> screaming.*

SVEN. Gurls.

> RUPERT *grins weakly.*

> Orlvoys. Du gurls.

> RUPERT *nods.*

> Orlvoys. Du charsink. Und du runnink. Vrom du gurls.

> RUPERT *twines the catgut in his fingers.*

> Bit vort kun a poor boy do?

ONEEYE *enters behind* SVEN. *He carries, before his face, a dartboard. Instead of the usual face, the poster-face of* SVEN, *hideously torn, six darts in it.* RUPERT *notices.* SVEN *turns.*

Vort –

Slight pause.

Und vort –

Slight pause.

Und vort ist da?

ONEEYE *throws down the dartboard.*

You!

ONEEYE. Yes, Svensson. Me.

He nods to RUPERT, *who pulls the catgut round* SVEN's *neck. Freeze, sound out, and* ONEEYE *out front.*

For who among us, for who among you, good people all, has not at some moment, from time to time, surreptitiously, nursed the desire to dismember Robert Redford, Paul McCartney, Steve MacQueen? And who among us has not, at some stage, off and on – secretly, nurtured the urge to mutilate Paul Newman, David Essex, and each Bee Gee? Savagely? Those who are beautiful and know it, those who are powerful and love it, those who are fashionable and have lost even the passion to desire it. Those who will take whatsoever things are violent, whatsoever things are base, whatsoever things are revolutionary and ugly, sexual and primitive, and they will sterilize these things, and they'll pollute them with their beauty, and they will wear them and play them on their eight-track stereo and they will frame them and hang them on their white-glossed walls and they'll accommodate the anger of these things, their power, they will drain them, make them pure. Those who will look at us with no reaction, no, not even scorn.

Pause.

There is a theory, spoken in quiet places, whispered in dark corners, that Karl Marx got it wrong. There is a concept, expressed in dirty leaflets, chalked on foggy walls, that it is not classes that divide the world. But beauty. Ugliness.

Pause.

AND ONE DAY. ONE DAY. WE'LL RISE. And, up and down the land, the boiled and warted wreak a horrible revenge. Then shall unlovely losers liquidate the latest faces, then shall the balding depilate the hirsute, and the weaklings, roving in wild mobs, kick sand in every eye; then ageing tailors run amok in dark boutiques and obese housewives butcher slimmers of the month. Then shall plump, acned groupies rise and slay the Osmond Brothers; starlets juggle with the severed limbs of stars, and stars will dance round smoking pyres of superstars; and secret wankers, formed in violent gangs, shall do destruction on the objects of their masturbation fantasies . . . And all the maimed, deformed and corpulent; the ugly, hare-lipped and incontinent; shall rise and seek, destroy, and will inherit all the earth.

Pause.

So then. And there. We killed Sven Svensson. Horribly.

Sounds of banging and screaming back as ONEEYE *helps* RUPERT *strangle* SVEN. *Sound of the door crashing in and blackout and silence.*

RUPERT (*whispers*). The door's broken, Oneeye.

ONEEYE (*whispers*). Yes, I know.

RUPERT (*whispers*). They'll come in, Oneeye.

ONEEYE (*whispers*). Yes, I know.

RUPERT (*whispers*). They'll see us, what we done here, Oneeye.

ONEEYE (*whispers*). Yes, I know.

Pause. Lights and screaming. ONEEYE *stands, one foot on* SVEN's *mangled body, in a hero's pose. We cannot tell if the screams are in horror or worship. Cut out.*

RUPERT. I think we got it wrong, Oneeye.

Blackout and 'The Ballad of a Thin Man', very loud.

End of Play.

BABY LOVE

Characters

A Catholic PRIEST
EILEEN MILLET – aged 20
SHAHID DAZ – aged 22
MRS TAYLOR – EILEEN's aunt, aged 47
DOCTOR – middle-aged
JANET HAIGH – aged 22
DETECTIVE – middle-aged
1st POLICEWOMAN
2nd POLICEWOMAN
COUNSEL for the prosecution
ASSISTANT GOVERNOR
WARDRESS
SILLITOE – psychologist, about 30
MRS O'BRIEN – Social Security investigator, aged 34
2nd WARDRESS

Doubling

For FIVE doubling as follows:
EILEEN
SHAHID
PRIEST/DOCTOR/DETECTIVE/COUNSEL/SILLITOE
MRS TAYLOR/1st POLICEWOMAN/WARDRESS
JANET/2nd POLICEWOMAN/MRS O'BRIEN/ASSISTANT
    GOVERNOR/2nd WARDRESS

Time and Setting

The main action takes place in an industrial town in the West
Riding of Yorkshire. Other scenes take place in Morecambe,
Lancashire; and a women's prison in England. The time is 1972.

Baby Love was first staged at Leeds Playhouse in on 16th March 1973. The cast was as follows:

EILEEN MILLET	Maureen Darbyshire
PRIEST, DOCTOR, DETECTIVE, COUNSEL	William Whymper
SHAHID DAZ	Peter Bourke
WARDRESS, ASSISTANT GOVERNOR	Elizabeth Bennett
JANET, 2nd POLICEWOMAN, 2nd WARDRESS	Irene Richard
MRS TAYLOR, MRS O'BRIEN	Vanessa Rosenthal
1st POLICEWOMAN	Amanda Jessel
SILLITOE	David Hatton

Directed by Jim Duckett
Designed by Robert Sandiford and Judith Wild
Stage Manager Duncan Wheeler

The play was first produced in London at the Soho Poly Theatre on 28th May 1973. The cast was as follows:

EILEEN MILLET	Patti Love
PRIEST, DOCTOR, DETECTIVE, COUNSEL, SILLITOE	Peter Miles
SHAHID DAZ	Madhav Sharma
JANET, 2nd POLICEWOMAN, MRS O'BRIEN, WARDRESS	Jenny Harrington
MRS TAYLOR, 1st POLICEWOMAN, ASSISTANT GOVERNOR, 2nd WARDRESS	Heather Chasen

Directed by James O'Brien
Designed by Sue Plummer
Stage Manager Bryan Saint Germain

The play was broadcast as a BBC Play for Today on 7 November 1974, directed by Barry Davis and produced by Kenith Trodd. The cast included Patti Love as Eileen, Donald Gee as Sillitoe, and Dev Sagoo as Shahid.

Prologue

Darkness. Church music playing softly. A single dim yellow light fades up on
EILEEN *and a Catholic* PRIEST. EILEEN, *in prison clothes, is sitting
untidily on a chair. The* PRIEST *stands. The grouping is stylised. Neither
looks at the other. The* PRIEST *speaks softly but urgently, as if in
confession.* EILEEN *is sullen, withdrawn, speaks in a West Riding accent.*

PRIEST. I ask you again. Do you truly repent?

> EILEEN *shrugs.*

> You know that unless you repent, your sin may not be
> absolved.

> *Pause.*

EILEEN (*with a small shrug*). Sin?

PRIEST. For the sinner not to know sin is but to compound his
wickedness.

> *Slight pause.*

EILEEN. If I'm that bad, why bother?

PRIEST. Because God teaches compassion.

EILEEN. What's that mean?

PRIEST. Love.

EILEEN. Oh.

> *Pause.*

> Like you have compassion for God?

PRIEST. No. Compassion is love for the sinner.

> *Pause.*

EILEEN. That sounds like pity.

PRIEST. God's mercy is infinite, and joy is there in heaven over
one lost sheep that repenteth, more than over ninety and
nine just persons that need no repentance.

EILEEN. I don't want pity. I don't see how love's wicked.

PRIEST. This was not love, but covetousness. Remember the commandment:

Lights and music begin to fade.

Thou shalt not covet thy neighbour's house, nor thy neighbour's wife, nor his manservant, nor his maidservant, nor his ox, nor his ass . . . nor his child . . .

Scene One

Darkness. Immediately, we hear a loud whimpering. It could be that of a baby – it is in fact EILEEN. *The crying goes on throughout this scene, a permanent background noise.*

The set is the living room of EILEEN's *small furnished flat. Two entrances – one into* EILEEN's *bedroom, the other into the hall. Off the hall is, we imagine, the kitchen and the lavatory. Sparse, tatty furniture. An armchair, an upright chair, and a table, on it a pub ashtray and dirty coffee mugs. A pram stands downstage of the main acting area of the scene.*

After a moment of whimpering, a match is lit on stage. The match lights a cigarette.

Lights up. The cigarette is SHAHID's. *He sits in the armchair, smoking. He is dressed in modern English clothes, not expensively, but in good taste. He is nervous and jumpy. After a moment, he stands, walks towards the bedroom door, thinks better of it, returns, sits again. He looks agitated at* EILEEN's *whimpering. Absent-mindedly he stubs the cigarette out, a nervous gesture. Realises what he's done, lights it again.*

A knock. SHAHID *rises, exits into the hall. We hear the outside door to the flat opened offstage.*

MRS TAYLOR (*off*). Oh. Is this . . .

SHAHID (*off*). Mrs Taylor?

MRS TAYLOR (*off*). Yes, I'm looking for Miss Millet . . .

SHAHID (*off*). Eileen's in here. Please come in.

Sound of door shutting. Enter MRS TAYLOR *followed by* SHAHID. MRS TAYLOR *is a genteel, lower-middle-class woman with a slight Yorkshire accent.*

MRS TAYLOR. Were you – did you just telephone me?

SHAHID. Yes.

Slight pause.

The doctor's here. He's with Eileen now.

MRS TAYLOR. Is that her making that dreadful noise?

SHAHID. The baby came three-quarters of an hour ago.

MRS TAYLOR. Alive?

SHAHID. Yes. But it is too small. I think it will die.

Pause.

It is good of you to come here.

MRS TAYLOR. I didn't even know. I had no idea where she lived or what had happened.

Pause.

She's making a terrible noise.

SHAHID. Would you like a cup of tea, coffee?

MRS TAYLOR. No. No thank you.

Pause.

Was the doctor here when the baby was born?

SHAHID. No. I had no idea what to do.

MRS TAYLOR. You were with her?

SHAHID. Yes. I had just come back from the telephone downstairs.

Slight pause.

It looked so small. Perfect. But so small.

Pause.

MRS TAYLOR. Look, I'm sorry, but who are you?

SHAHID. Who am I?

MRS TAYLOR. I mean – what are you – what's your position –

SHAHID. You mean, what is my position in relation to Eileen?

MRS TAYLOR. Yes.

SHAHID. In English – the words are very difficult. You cannot say it without a moral sting.

Pause.

MRS TAYLOR. I suppose by that you mean that she is your mistress.

SHAHID. You see?

Pause.

MRS TAYLOR. And this baby?

SHAHID (*shrugs, it's obvious*). Ours.

MRS TAYLOR. You and Eileen?

SHAHID. Is that so bad?

Enter the DOCTOR *from the bedroom. He is not wearing his jacket, his shirt-sleeves are rolled up, his tie loosened, his hands bloody.* SHAHID *and* MRS TAYLOR *look at him.*

DOCTOR. The baby died two minutes ago, I'm afraid.

SHAHID *quickly moves towards the bedroom door.*

No. Leave her for the moment. I've given her a shot. It should make her sleep.

SHAHID. I want to see her.

DOCTOR. Not now. Please.

SHAHID *shrugs.*

MRS TAYLOR. Doctor, I'm Eileen's aunt, is there anything . . .?

DOCTOR. Not at present, thank you, Mrs . . .

MRS TAYLOR. Taylor.

DOCTOR. Not at present, Mrs Taylor.

Looks at his hands.

Excuse me. Wash.

Exit into the hall. Pause.

MRS TAYLOR. Why wasn't he here?

SHAHID. When?

MRS TAYLOR. When the baby was born.

SHAHID (*a note of anger*). Because the ambulance will not come unless they are told to by a doctor or a hospital. And Eileen's doctor doesn't work at night. So this doctor had to come from Leeds.

Pause.

It was only just over thirty minutes, you see, from the pains starting.

Looks at his watch.

And not much more until it is dead.

MRS TAYLOR. It must have been terrible for her. To have it, here. Like this. Dreadful.

Pause.

SHAHID. When it first came, it was quite still, for half a minute at least, it lay there. Eileen, you understand, she couldn't see it, obviously, and she kept asking, is it alive, is it alive. And I thought it was dead, but I didn't know, so I said, yes, it is alive, it breathes, and then suddenly it gave a kind of jerk and began to cry. But it wasn't a healthy cry. And now it is dead.

Pause.

MRS TAYLOR. Well, in one way, I suppose . . .

Slight pause.

SHAHID (*slightly threatening*). What do you suppose, in one way?

MRS TAYLOR. No, perhaps I didn't mean that.

SHAHID. You mean you suppose it is all for the best, in one way?

MRS TAYLOR. No, I didn't say that, what I meant was . . .

She gestures vaguely round the room.

She couldn't support a child. Could she? Unmarried, no job.

SHAHID. And, of course, it wasn't white.

Pause.

That's what you were thinking. It doesn't matter if it dies, this coffee-coloured baby, so much as if it was white. Yes?

MRS TAYLOR. I didn't say –

SHAHID. That is what you meant, I think.

Slight pause.

MRS TAYLOR. Yes, I think that is what I meant. However old-fashioned it may sound to you.

Pause.

However – passe.

Pause.

Her mother would be heartbroken if she knew.

SHAHID. She does know.

MRS TAYLOR. What?

SHAHID. I telephoned her. Before I telephoned you. She has not spoken with Eileen since Eileen said she was pregnant. I tell her that Eileen is very ill. That Eileen is asking for her. She puts down the telephone. So. Heartbroken.

MRS TAYLOR. I don't think you could understand her point of view.

SHAHID. No.

Pause.

MRS TAYLOR. I wish she'd stop crying.

Enter the DOCTOR *from the hall. He gives a perfunctory half-smile to* MRS TAYLOR *before going through into the bedroom.*

SHAHID. If it pleases you, Eileen and I are no longer together.

MRS TAYLOR. Oh. I see. As soon as you've made her pregnant, you walk out on her.

SHAHID. No. We don't see each other because if we are

together, here, your famous English Welfare State says that
we are as man and wife and gives Eileen no money. That is
why we do not see each other.

Slight pause.

MRS TAYLOR. Then why are you here?

SHAHID. She felt ill. There was no-one else. So she telephoned
me at the club where I work. By then she knew it was the
baby coming. So I went to telephone the doctor, her mother
and you.

MRS TAYLOR. I see.

*Enter the DOCTOR from the bedroom. He carries his jacket and bag.
He puts the bag on the table, opens it, takes out a pad, starts writing
something.*

DOCTOR (*to MRS TAYLOR*). This is a note confirming the
baby's death. You must take it to the Registrar of Births,
Marriages and Deaths so they can fill in Birth and Death
Certificates for the child.

SHAHID. But it was only alive for an hour.

DOCTOR. That doesn't matter.

*He finishes writing, tears the note off the pad, offers it to MRS
TAYLOR.*

SHAHID. I will do it.

SHAHID *takes the note from the DOCTOR.*

MRS TAYLOR. It's all right, I . . .

SHAHID. You need not trouble. I will do it.

He puts the note in his trouser pocket.

I wish to see Eileen now.

DOCTOR. You may as well. She's not going to sleep.

SHAHID *exits into bedroom.* EILEEN's *whimpering dies down a
little during the following dialogue.* DOCTOR *takes a packet of
cigarettes from his jacket, offers one to* MRS TAYLOR. *She shakes her
head. He lights his cigarette.*

DOCTOR. Attractive girl. Bright. Pity.

MRS TAYLOR. Yes.

Pause.

DOCTOR. Why don't they leave off it, eh? If they can't be bothered with precautions. Still, the age we live in.

MRS TAYLOR. She comes from a good home.

DOCTOR. It must be upsetting for you, seeing her in this state.

Slight pause. DOCTOR *rolling down his sleeves.*

What a mess they get themselves into. When they know it all.

MRS TAYLOR. You weren't here when it happened?

DOCTOR (*tying his tie*). At the birth? No. I'm coupled with Eileen's doctor here. The coloured boy rang him up and was redirected to me. It's not a perfect system, but we can't all work 24 hours every day.

MRS TAYLOR. Do you think it might have been saved?

DOCTOR. There's always a chance. But – I think – I doubt it. Then again, seven and a half months, no deformities . . .

Pause. MRS TAYLOR *looks round the room.*

Does she work?

MRS TAYLOR. She had a job in a carpet factory. Why, I don't know. She was a clever girl, been to college. But lazy. She lost the job over something, I can't remember. Since then, unemployed. Apparently she's had trouble getting her benefits.

DOCTOR. Yes.

EILEEN'*s crying rises again. Enter* SHAHID *quickly from the bedroom.*

SHAHID. Doctor, she's in great pain, can't you give her something . . .

DOCTOR. There's nothing I can do.

SHAHID. But she's in terrible –

The whimpering stops suddenly. They ALL *look towards the bedroom door. Enter* EILEEN. *She wears a night-dress. She is holding the dead baby, wrapped in a towel. She looks manic, holding the baby's body to her, protecting it from attack. She runs to the pram, whips round, still glaring at everyone. Then she lays the body in the pram, immediately turning back to stand facing the* OTHERS, *protecting the pram from them. Then suddenly, she puts her hand to her mouth, about to be sick. She runs into the hall. Sound of the lavatory door slamming and* EILEEN *being sick. No-one else moves. A long pause.*

SHAHID. She wanted that child, doctor. It's not true what you think. Either of you. She wanted to have a baby of her own and to be its mother.

Pause.

DOCTOR (*slight shrug*). She bought a pram, even –

Snap blackout.

Scene Two

A single light fades up on the pram, in the same position as in the last scene. EILEEN *stands by the pram. She wears a long military-style blue overcoat. She is looking into the pram. A pause.*

EILEEN. Oh. There y'are. Where've you been? Just woken up, have you? Come on, then. Up you come.

She lifts a baby from the pram.

I'm back now. That's right. Eh, you want a hug, don't you? Course you do. You want a cuddle.

She cuddles the baby.

Who's a daft one, then? My little baby.

Pause.

No crying now. No.

Pause.

My little baby, 'cos you love me, eh? So much eh?

Pause.

Love you so much.

Snap blackout and tape of police siren. Then fade tape out and fade up a corridor of light at the front of the stage, taking in the pram, and JANET, who stands a few feet away from it. She is nervous, upset, near to cracking, but determined to be helpful. She talks to imaginary people in front of her, out of the lights, blinking and shielding her eyes from time to time to see them better. In most of her pauses, we imagine that she has been asked a question.

JANET. It was here.

She goes to the pram.

I left the pram here. It was only for a minute.

Pause.

Oh, I can't . . . not more than two minutes, I'm sure. I mean, I wouldn't, not for . . .

Pause.

It was very crowded, you see . . . I couldn't have taken the pram into the shop, and I only wanted . . . just to buy a magazine . . .

Slight pause. Then an insistent after-thought.

You see, with there being so many people, really thought, I mean, there were people everywhere, it's a pedestrian precinct . . . I didn't think anyone could have . . .

Pause. She doesn't catch a question.

I'm sorry?

Pause.

Yes, of course, as soon as I came out of the shop I looked in the pram to see if he was all right, and then I saw that he . . .

She is upset.

No, it's all right, really . . .

Pause.

What?

Pause.

For the television?

Pause.

You mean, to whoever took Simon?

Pause.

You mean, what would I like to tell them?

Pause.

Oh, I don't . . . it's difficult to know what to . . .

Pause.

Oh, all right. What do I . . . ?

An imaginary someone indicates that she should move to face a camera.

Oh, yes.

She moves slightly, faces into an imaginary camera.

Here?

Pause.

Right. Do you want me to . . . ?

Pause.

Right.

Slight pause.

Yes, I'm ready.

Pause. She is given a signal.

Well –

Snap blackout.

Scene Three

At once, JANET's voice on tape. In the darkness, set up two areas. One is a small furnished room in Morecambe, EILEEN's room. The pram is in this area. A television set faces upstage, on top of it, a paper bag of apples. A suitcase lies on the floor, also EILEEN's overcoat. Opposite the TV set, facing downstage, is a large armchair.

The other area is an interview room in a police station. Two chairs, either side of a table. SHAHID *sits. These two areas are lit independently.*

JANET's *voice.* My name is Janet Haigh. I am 22 years old, and today someone stole my four-month-old baby Simon from outside a shop near to where I live. I don't know if whoever did take Simon is watching this, but if they are, I'd just like to say that if they had any idea, any idea at all, what this thing has done to me and my husband, I'm sure that whatever their feelings they'd let us have him back.

The flickering light of the TV set slowly fades up, so we see EILEEN *watching it as she sprawls in the armchair, eating an apple. When the TV light is up, fade up general lights on* EILEEN's *area. During this sequence,* EILEEN *watches as if what was going on was nothing to do with her. She instinctively dislikes* JANET's *manner and vocabulary, and reacts accordingly, but as one would to a politician on television, objectively.* JANET's *voice continues as the lights come up.*

JANET's *voice.* Perhaps the person who stole my baby hasn't got a baby of their own. I don't know. But if they haven't then they can't understand what we feel having lost ours so suddenly.

EILEEN *scratches her stomach.*

I know that this sort of thing has happened before, and although I'm not, we're not clever people . . .

EILEEN. Huh.

JANET's *voice.* . . . we know that it's not really a crime, that people who do this are ill, through no fault of their own.

EILEEN *pulls a face.*

But you must understand, if you're watching this, whoever you are, that although we're very sympathetic with you if you've got lots of troubles . . .

EILEEN *pulls a face.*

. . . our main concern is to find our baby and even if you do have troubles and problems I can't see how taking Simon's going to help, really, in the long run, because you must be found out eventually. I don't see how it helps.

EILEEN. No, I'll bet.

The baby, in the pram, begins to cry softly.

JANET's *voice*. Perhaps if I told you a bit about ourselves, it might help you to understand.

EILEEN. Oh, yeh.

Turns to pram.

Shh.

JANET's *voice*. My husband Paul and I have been married for 18 months and the one thing we always really wanted was to have a baby of our very own.

EILEEN *looks to heaven, then speaks to pram.*

EILEEN. Shh, love.

JANET's *voice*. It was the one thing we wanted to have more than anything else in the whole world.

EILEEN *plays imaginary violin, humming a phrase of 'Hearts and Flowers'.*

And when I knew that I was going to have Simon, it was the happiest day of my life. And when the day came for him to be born – well, you can't imagine how I felt.

EILEEN (*standing up*). Too right I can't.

She takes another apple, sits. The baby's crying is getting louder.

JANET's *voice*. And then for it all to be suddenly shattered, all to be suddenly shattered, all that joy . . .

EILEEN (*to the pram*). Shh.

JANET's *voice has paused*. EILEEN *looks questioningly at the TV set.*

JANET's *voice*. I don't think I can say any more.

EILEEN. Aw, go on . . . force yourself.

JANET's *voice*. Only that – if you are watching, whoever you are – just to say that you've broken our hearts.

EILEEN. Aw, bloody real.

She throws the apple core vaguely behind her.

LINKMAN's *voice*. Mrs Janet Haigh, mother of four-month-old baby-snatch victim Simon Haigh, speaking earlier today. That report came from Leeds. And now, on a lighter note, we meet a Blackburn man who claims the world record for keeping a live piranha fish down his trousers . . .

EILEEN *switches the television off, and immediately goes to the pram.*

EILEEN. Look, shut up, will you?

Baby still crying.

Aw . . .

She picks the baby out of the pram.

Come on, shh, shh . . . your mam's here, Nikky, mam's here, don't cry . . .

Baby still crying.

Aw, come on, love, quiet . . .

Pause.

D'you want feeding? Do you? Are you hungry, love?

Baby still crying.

All right, I'll feed you. You've had a long day, what with the chuff-chuff and all, eh?

She puts the baby back in the pram.

Hold on, tea's coming.

She goes to the suitcase, opens it, rummages about, finds two tins of baby food, puts them down, rummages again, finds a spoon and a tin-opener, both wrapped in tissue paper.

See? Whose clever mam got a tin-opener? You thought she'd forget, didn't you, and we'd be right up creek without paddle.

She is opening a tin, slips, cuts herself.

Shit.

She looks guiltily in the baby's direction. Then smiles, shrugs. Finishes opening the tin. The baby still crying. EILEEN puts the open tin on the floor by the armchair, goes and gets the baby, still crying, and carries it to the armchair. She sits on the arm of the armchair, picks up the tin and the spoon, starts trying to feed the baby, whose crying gets less.

Ooh, you are a dribbler, aren't you?

She reaches over to the suitcase and finds a flannel, wipes the baby's face.

There y'are. Now come on. Eat up like a good boy.

In disgust.

Ooh, what a mess. You don't want it, do you? Making a noise fit to wake the dead, and you're not hungry, are you?

Pause. Baby crying.

Are you?

She puts the tin and the spoon down, stands, holding the baby.

I think I'm going to have to consult my little book about you.

She puts the baby back in the pram, still crying.

Shhh.

She goes to the suitcase, kneels by it, finds a babycare book, opens it, reads.

'What Father Can Do'. Ha Ha.

Reads something else.

Oh God. Milk.

Calls to the baby.

It's milk you're wanting, in't it? And whose clever mam forgot to get any. Baby's egg and bacon breakfast, rusks by ton, but no bloody milk.

She looks at her watch.

And it's way past shops. Oh, I'm sorry, pet.

She looks at the book. Sudden surprise.

Oh, course. Why not? Nature to rescue.

She stands, still holding the book, then a thought, she looks disturbed.

Oh, but you . . . if you're not . . .

Pause. Baby still crying. Happier.

Oh, well, wet nurses do, don't they? And you are. Really. Aren't you?

EILEEN *reads from the book, in a mock posh voice.*

'How To Hold Baby At The Breast'.

She shuts the suitcase, puts it next to the armchair, lays the book open on it, so she can consult it.

Won't be a minute, love.

EILEEN *takes off her sweater, unhooks her bra, and takes down one shoulder strap, so that one breast is free. She looks at her breast, feels it, looks at the book – in which, we assume, is an illustration – and shrugs.*

Well, we can't all be . . . Rachel Welsh.

She goes and picks the crying baby up, returns to the armchair, sits on its arm.

Right, chuck, are you going to get a mouthful.

She looks down at the book and humps the baby into the right position, then holds the baby to her breast. Pause. She looks down.

Come on, suck.

Holds baby close again. The baby still whimpering.

Look, pet, suck, damn you.

Holds the baby up in front of her face.

Look, I want you to suck. Like this.

She sucks.

See?

She sucks again.

Suck.

She puts the baby back to her breast. The baby stops crying.

That's better. Who's a good little boy, then. Have as much as you want. 'S'all free.

Baby starts crying again.

Oh, Jesus.

EILEEN *holds the baby up.*

What's the matter now, eh?

A thought. She puts the baby on her lap, feels her breast.

I don't think I've got any. None there. Shh, Nikky, shh.

She looks down at the book, reaches down, turns a page.

Oh. Stimulate.

She tries to stimulate her nipple, still looking at the book. Then gives up.

Well, I'm sorry, chuck, but it looks like udder's empty.

Slight pause.

Eh, I wonder if it matters which one?

She looks at the book, shrugs. Then to baby.

Hold on, kid, I'm transferring you, for an undisclosed fee, to me other udder.

She adjusts her bra, freeing the other breast, puts the baby to her breast.

Right. Have a good pull at this one (*She feels her breast.*)

Pause.

Dry as a bone.

Baby's crying intensifies. Tenderly.

Oh, don't cry. Don't cry, pet.

Holds the baby to her, kisses it.

Don't cry.

The baby's crying reduces to a whimper. EILEEN lays the baby in her lap, begins to do up her bra.

That's better. Now I'll go out and try and find a shop that's open, eh? Get some milk. Happen there's a machine, p'raps. Y'all right? Five minutes? Are you? Is little Nikky most beautiful one? Is he?

Slight pause. She picks the baby up.

Oh, God. You've been doing your business again, haven't you? You're all squashy. Yurrgh.

Baby cries loudly. EILEEN stands with baby.

Oh, all right, I'll change you. Don't start all that again . . .

Baby crying.

Nikky, you'll drive me daft if you keep on like this.

Pause, Baby cries. EILEEN *angry.*

Look, you little beast, will you *shut up!*

The baby stops crying. Then cut out lights on EILEEN's *area and lights up on Police Station area. During following sequence,* EILEEN *puts the baby in the pram, exits, re-enters dressed, sets up clothes horse with nappies and her own clothes, unpacks suitcase, leaving room covered with baby food and paraphernalia. By the end of this sequence,* EILEEN *has taken the baby out of the pram and is sitting in the armchair, feeding it milk from a bottle. In the police station area, enter a* DETECTIVE, *carrying a clipboard. He sees* SHAHID.

DETECTIVE (*reading from his clipboard, pronouncing badly and with difficulty*). Sha-hid Daz?

SHAHID. That's right.

DETECTIVE (*sitting down opposite* SHAHID). Waiter and graduate of Huddersfield Polytechnic.

SHAHID. Yes.

DETECTIVE. Well, well. Now, what's all this about?

SHAHID. I want to report a missing person.

DETECTIVE. Yes, I know all that.

Pause. DETECTIVE *looking at* SHAHID.

SHAHID. Well, that's it. I want to report that this person is missing.

DETECTIVE. Why?

SHAHID. Why?

DETECTIVE. A kid's moved on. Changed her address. Any number of possible reasons. Why tell us?

SHAHID. Because I'm worried about her.

DETECTIVE (*in surprise*). Oh. And why's that?

SHAHID. Well, do you expect people suddenly to disappear off the face of the earth?

DETECTIVE (*shrugs*). Young girl, living in a bedsit, unemployed, moving on all the time, that sort are.

SHAHID. Also, she is not well. Two months ago, she lost her baby.

DETECTIVE. Oh. And who told us that?

SHAHID. We didn't need telling.

DETECTIVE. Oh, I see. Indeed.

Pause.

Well, we won't say owt about that, eh? Now, we have her here as 20, right?

SHAHID. About 20.

DETECTIVE. You don't know?

SHAHID. Not exactly.

DETECTIVE. Jesus.

(*NOTE: Change following to suit actress.*)

She's approximately five foot six, thin, short, curly blonde hair, oval-shaped face, pale complexion, brown eyes, thin nose, slightly turned up. Last seen . . . oh, we've not got this. D'you know what kind of coat she usually wears?

SHAHID. Oh . . . she has the one, only, I think. It's a kind of army coat, you know? Long. Blue. With silver buttons.

DETECTIVE (*surprised*). Right. Long blue army-type overcoat with silver buttons.

Something stirs in the back of the DETECTIVE's *mind. He sits stock still, thinking. Then, quite quietly.*

Bloody hell.

Suddenly stands.

SHAHID. What's . . . ?

DETECTIVE. Just stay right there. Don't move.

Exit DETECTIVE.

SHAHID. Why?

Slight pause. Re-enter DETECTIVE *with a sheet of paper.*

DETECTIVE (*reads*). About five foot five inches. Thin. Wavy blonde hair. Brown eyes. Wearing a blue full-length overcoat, military greatcoat style.

SHAHID. Yes?

DETECTIVE. Right, mate. You and I are going to have a talk.

SHAHID. I thought you had all the information you needed.

DETECTIVE (*sitting down*). Not by a long stretch, son. Now. Your lady friend's name is Eileen Millet, right?

SHAHID. Yes.

DETECTIVE. And you last saw her a week ago.

SHAHID. That's right. But I don't see . . .

DETECTIVE. Just answer the questions, son. Now, have you any idea where she might have gone. Any places where she's got friends, here or anywhere else. Any aunts, cousins, anything like that.

SHAHID. Well, her aunt lives round here, apart from that –

DETECTIVE. Right, we'll have her address. And the parents?

SHAHID. I have their telephone number, but they won't –

DETECTIVE (*writing*). Good . . . Now anyone else, at all? Friends from work, she might go and stay with?

SHAHID. She is no longer in work.

DETECTIVE. Well, any friends she had when she was at work?

SHAHID. No, she didn't get on too well there.

DETECTIVE. Any other friends?

SHAHID. All that I know, I have visited, looking for her.

DETECTIVE. Holidays? Where does she go for her holidays?

SHAHID. Oh, last year, I think, she went to, where is it? On the coast of Lancashire.

DETECTIVE. Blackpool?

SHAHID. No . . .

DETECTIVE. Morecambe?

SHAHID. Yes, that's it. Morecambe. She used to go there every summer.

DETECTIVE (*stands, paces about, to himself*). Young girl, on her own, moves into digs or a bedsit or a flat in the last few days with a small baby . . .

SHAHID. What?

DETECTIVE. Possibly here, possibly Morecambe, could be bloody anywhere.

SHAHID. A baby?

DETECTIVE (*suddenly, snaps his fingers*). Orange juice.

SHAHID. I'm sorry?

DETECTIVE (*to SHAHID, as if it was obvious*). They give them bloody orange juice. The Welfare people.

SHAHID. Please, what is going on . . .

DETECTIVE. Right, lad, come with me.

SHAHID. Haven't you finished?

DETECTIVE. No we have not.

He strides out, SHAHID *following.*

SHAHID (*as he goes*). But she has no baby . . .

Cross-cut lights back to EILEEN's *area.* EILEEN *sitting in the armchair, feeding the baby and talking to it.*

EILEEN. Drink up, now, pet, drink up like a good boy, make you strong, baby.

Pause.

Tell you a story? True story. Birth in a backroom. Your birth, baby.

Slight pause.

Eh, you know, you're meant to see Virgin Mary as you look up from bearing, d'you know that? I were told. Look up, when you're bearing, and you'll see the Blessed Virgin, holding Gentle Jesus.

Slight pause.

Didn't see no Virgin Mary when I threw you up, Nikky.
You'll not guess what I saw.

Slight pause.

A stork, I saw, with a corpse in its beak, smashing its torn
feet at the glass of the window . . .

Pause.

Go out tomorrow, eh? If 's sunny.

Pause.

And d'you know, I thought you were dead then. Aye. I cried
and cried for all that hurting I'd had, you need a lot of love
to hurt that much, Nikky; with a bloody dead thing on
mattress, too much to bear.

Pause.

You're so pale now. Paler than I thought. Go out tomorrow.
Get you some sun. Get you some colour.

Pause.

Went out looking. Loved too much to lose you. So went out
looking like shepherd for his one lost lamb . . . Loved you
enough to find you again when I thought you were lost,
baby. Loved you more than just for bearing, loved you for
looking and finding.

Slight pause.

Loved you enough to keep you, Nikky?

Pause.

Go out tomorrow?

Cross-out lights back to Police Station. EILEEN *stays where she is.
We discover the* DETECTIVE *and a* POLICEWOMAN. *He is
putting down the telephone.*

DETECTIVE. That's it. Trying to pick up her SS. Thank God for
the Welfare State.

He stands.

We'll nip over and pick her up.

Cross-cut lights back to EILEEN's *room,* EILEEN *stands, with the baby.* DETECTIVE *exits.*

EILEEN. Right. Decided. We go out tomorrow. Now time for your nap.

A door bell rings as EILEEN *puts the baby in the pram. She goes and looks down out of an imaginary window in the fourth wall. Then panics.*

Christ it's cops.

Bell rings again.

Oh God I hope no-one's in.

Sound of the front door, downstairs, opening.

Oh God I bet it's that stupid old bag downstairs letting 'em in. Oh Christ.

She rushes round the room picking up nappies, baby food, etc. When she has collected all she can see, she stands holding it, looking round, not knowing what to do. Then an idea. She puts all that she's holding into the pram.

No, no, be quiet, pet, please be quiet just this once.

A knock on EILEEN's *door. A look of panic on her face. She notices another nappy on the floor, picks it up, throws it in the pram. Then looks round again. Another knock.* EILEEN *looks desperate. She pushes the pram offstage – not the main exit of the room – we imagine into another room or a cupboard. Another knock.* EILEEN *re-enters. Stands. Doesn't move. Another knock.* EILEEN *whispers.*

Oh go away. Please go away.

DETECTIVE (*off*). I'll have to break it.

EILEEN *look of panic. Sound of someone charging the door.* EILEEN *cannot move. Again the sound of someone charging the door.*

EILEEN (*suddenly*). All right, all right, I'm coming.

She kicks her shoes off, ruffles her hair, rushes out. Sound of a door opening.

EILEEN (*yawning*). Hallo, what is it? I were asleep.

DETECTIVE (*off*). Eileen Millet?

Slightest pause.

EILEEN (*off*). No, I'm sorry, I think you've got the wrong . . .

DETECTIVE (*off*). As you can see, we're police officers. We'd like a word with you.

EILEEN (*off*). But I'm not Eileen – whoever. Really.

DETECTIVE (*off*). We'd like a word with you just the same.

Pause.

Thank you.

Enter DETECTIVE, *two* POLICEWOMEN, *and* EILEEN.

EILEEN (*putting her shoes on, acting badly*). What's all this about, then?

DETECTIVE *looking round the room.*

1st POLICEWOMAN. We have reason to believe you have a baby here.

EILEEN. A baby? No. Not me.

1st POLICEWOMAN. Are you sure?

EILEEN. Oh, quite sure.

DETECTIVE. Look, love, drop it, will you? We know who you are, and the old girl downstairs confirmed about the baby. So where is it?

EILEEN (*quickly*). There's a baby in one of other flats, over corridor. That's baby she meant.

DETECTIVE *picks up* EILEEN's *babycare book from the floor.*

DETECTIVE. A little light general reading? (*To* 2nd POLICEWOMAN.) Find it.

EILEEN *rushes at* 2nd POLICEWOMAN, *attacks her.*

EILEEN. No! No! Leave us alone! Leave us alone!

1st POLICEWOMAN *grabs* EILEEN *from behind, holds her.* EILEEN *kicks and screams.* 2nd POLICEWOMAN *exits.*

EILEEN. Get off me! Get off me, you fucking pig! Get off me, you fucking cunt!

DETECTIVE. Clearly a well-bred young lady.

Enter 2nd POLICEWOMAN, *holding baby.*

2nd POLICEWOMAN. Here it is.

EILEEN. That's not your baby!

> EILEEN *breaks free from* 1st POLICEWOMAN, *and, taking her unawares, hits* 2nd POLICEWOMAN *and grabs the baby who starts screaming.* EILEEN *takes a cushion from the armchair, holds it in front of the baby's face. Not against it. The two* POLICEWOMEN *are about to go for* EILEEN.

DETECTIVE. Hold it! Eileen Jane Millet, I have to inform you –

1st POLICEWOMAN. Oh –

DETECTIVE (*covering, firmly*). I have to inform you that you are under arrest. You do not have to say anything, but anything you do say will be taken down and may be used in evidence against you. Right, love, hand it over.

EILEEN. He's not yours. You keep off. He's not yours.

1st POLICEWOMAN. Come on, Eileen. It's not yours either. You can't keep it.

EILEEN. He *is*! He's my baby. And if you – if you take one step towards me – just one step – I'll smother him – I promise you – I'll smother him.

DETECTIVE. Can't you hear it crying, love? You don't want it to cry. Give it to one of the lady policemen.

EILEEN. I've told you. I'll smother him.

2nd POLICEWOMAN. Come on, Eileen, you don't want to kill it. An innocent little baby. What's it done to you?

EILEEN. You'll kill him if I let you have him.

1st POLICEWOMAN. Don't be silly, Eileen, why would we want to do that?

EILEEN. You'll kill me too. I know.

2nd POLICEWOMAN. Now you know you're just being silly. We won't hurt it. We promise.

EILEEN. He doesn't want you to have him. He only wants me. He loves me. He's mine.

DETECTIVE. That baby isn't yours, love. It belongs to somebody else. NOW!

The POLICEWOMEN *go for* EILEEN, 2nd POLICEWOMAN
taking the baby, 1st POLICEWOMAN *securing* EILEEN, *who
kicks.*

1st POLICEWOMAN (*viciously*). Now – calm – down – Eileen – or
– I'll – have – to – get – rough – with – you.

EILEEN. Fuck off! Fuck off all of you! Fuck off!

1st POLICEWOMAN *swings* EILEEN *round and slaps her.*
EILEEN *looks for a moment as if she's going to hit back, then thinks
better of it, calms down.*

DETECTIVE. Right. Now we're all going away. You and us and
the baby. Right? All going away.

EILEEN (*quietly*). Fucking bastard coppers.

DETECTIVE. Come on, love.

DETECTIVE *leads* EILEEN *out.*

EILEEN (*as she goes, quietly*). Fucking bastard coppers.

They are gone. 1st POLICEWOMAN *putting clothes into*
EILEEN's *suitcase.*

2nd POLICEWOMAN (*to baby*). Shh, now, shh, baby. (*To* 1st
POLICEWOMAN.) She had it under a great pile of stuff in
there. It's a wonder it didn't suffocate there and then. Shh,
baby.

1st POLICEWOMAN. Stupid bitch.

EILEEN (*off, a scream*). Fucking bastard coppers stole my baby!

Sound of DETECTIVE *hitting* EILEEN.

2nd POLICEWOMAN. Kid gloves?

1st POLICEWOMAN. I'd have kicked her teeth in. But then I got
a kid too.

Exit 1st POLICEWOMAN *with* EILEEN's *suitcase.* 2nd
POLICEWOMAN *looks after her a moment, then to the baby.*

2nd POLICEWOMAN. Shh, baby. All over now.

Fade to blackout.

Scene Four

At once, a VOICE on tape, booming through an echo chamber. During this, Scene Three's sets are struck. Darkness.

VOICE. Eileen Jane Millet, you are charged with an offence of child-stealing, contrary to section 56 of the Offences Against the Person Act 1861. The particulars are that you, Eileen Jane Millet, on the 2nd day of May 1972, by force took away Simon Benedict Haigh, a child of the age of 17 weeks, with intent to deprive Nicholas John Haigh, the father of the said child, of the possession of the said child.

The words 'possession of the said child' are taken up with the echo and repeated, louder and louder. Then tape snaps out, and a spot comes up on JANET, standing on one side of the stage, holding the baby.

JANET. The nightmare's over now. It's been the most terrible two weeks of my life, but now I've got my baby again and everything's wonderful.

JANET's spot out. Spot on a COUNSEL, centre stage, wearing barrister's wig and gown.

COUNSEL. The offence with which the accused is charged took place on the morning of the 2nd of May this year. The accused, Eileen Jane Millet, who is 20 years of age, had suffered a miscarriage on the 12th of March which had, apparently, left her in a condition of some emotional distress.

COUNSEL's spot out. Spot on EILEEN standing on the opposite side of the stage to JANET. After a pause, she sings, slowly, weakly, sadly.

EILEEN. Anyone who had a

Slight pause.

heart, would look at

Slight pause.

me

Pause. Then EILEEN's spot out, JANET's spot on.

JANET. After all the heartbreak, we can both of us forget this dreadful thing we've been through.

JANET's spot off, COUNSEL's *spot on.*

COUNSEL. It was, in point of fact, two days after the date on which her baby would have been due that Millet, who was wandering aimlessly round the town centre, noticed an untended pram standing outside W.H. Smith's, the newsagents.

COUNSEL's *spot off,* EILEEN's *spot on.*

EILEEN *(still singing slowly and sadly).* Eleanor Rigby sits in the church

Stops, pause, corrects herself.

Eleanor Rigby picks up the rice

Slight pause.

in the church where the wedding has been

Longer pause.

Lives in a dream

EILEEN's *spot off,* JANET's *spot on.*

JANET. Already, it seems just like a bad dream. Simon is back in his own home, our home that was incomplete without him.

JANET's *spot out,* COUNSEL's *spot on.*

COUNSEL. The pram had been left there by Mrs Janet Haigh, who had entered the shop to purchase a magazine. In the pram was her baby Simon.

COUNSEL's *spot off,* EILEEN's *spot on.*

EILEEN *(still singing, slowly and sadly).* Goodbye

Slight pause.

Ruby Tuesday

Slight pause.

who could hang a name

Slight pause.

on you, when you change with

Long pause.

still I'm going to miss you

EILEEN*'s spot out,* JANET*'s spot on.*

JANET. I know he missed me. You can see how happy he is now
he's back with his own things. His own toys. In his own
mummy's and daddy's little nest. Which they built for him.

JANET*'s spot out,* COUNSEL*'s spot on.*

COUNSEL. Millet looked in the pram, and saw Simon lying
there. She then took the baby from the pram, and –

COUNSEL*'s spot out,* EILEEN*'s spot on.*

EILEEN (*sings, even slower*). Baby love

Pause.

my baby love

Pause.

I need you

Long pause.

oh how I need you

EILEEN *freeze, hold spot.* JANET*'s spot on.*

JANET. I know people like that need help. But I don't think we
could ever forgive her. But we hope to forget. After all, it was
stealing, just as if she'd taken our car or anything. She did
take something which belonged to us. But they shouldn't
have –

JANET *freeze, hold spot.* COUNSEL*'s spot on.* WARDRESS *enters
to him, takes his wig and gown, gives him a Judge's wig and robe,
which he puts on. Exit* WARDRESS.

COUNSEL (*takes a step forward*). Eileen Jane Millet, you have
pleaded guilty to an extremely serious offence. Your actions
caused unimaginable distress to the parents of the child you
stole, and taking that factor alone into account would lead
the court to impose a severe sentence. However, it is true
that your crime was the result of a personal tragedy, and
while this in no way mitigates the seriousness, and the
heartlessness of the offence, it is right, I believe, to exercise
leniency. The sentence of the court, therefore, is that you go

to prison for nine months. And it is to be hoped that you will take full benefit from those medical services which are provided in prison for your rehabilitation.

COUNSEL's *spot out and exit* COUNSEL. WARDRESS *moves into* EILEEN's *spot as she sings, very softly.*

EILEEN. Baby love, my baby love

Pause.

I need you

Pause.

Oh how I

WARDRESS. Time to go. Time to go, now.

WARDRESS *leads* EILEEN *out as her spot fades.* JANET *cuddles her baby.*

JANET. Back home. Baby back home, where baby belongs.

Pause. Then to audience, suddenly strong.

They should have helped her. Somehow. They shouldn't have shut her away.

Snap blackout.

Scene Five

A cold, hard light snaps up on stage. A table, on it a telephone, an ashtray and a bellpush, behind it a chair. Another chair to the side. The ASSISTANT GOVERNOR *enters and sits. Enter* SILLITOE, *carrying a file. He is youngish, pleasant and sincere. The atmosphere is immediately difficult.*

ASST. GOVERNOR. Dr Sillitoe?

SILLITOE. That's right. How do you do?

ASST. GOVERNOR. Well, thank you. Please sit down.

SILLITOE (*sitting*). Thank you.

ASST. GOVERNOR *picking up a letter on her desk.*

ASST. GOVERNOR. Now I gather that in their infinite wisdom the H.O. consider that you are better able to cope with our prisoners than we are.

SILLITOE. I wouldn't put it quite like that . . .

ASST. GOVERNOR. Quite how would you put it?

SILLITOE. I'd say that it's worth trying a different approach. In this one case. A second opinion, if you like.

ASST. GOVERNOR. Yes.

Pause.

Have you read our resident psychoanalyst's report?

SILLITOE *taking a file from his briefcase.*

SILLITOE. Yes, I have.

ASST. GOVERNOR. I assume you find it woefully inadequate.

SILLITOE. I think it – I understand fully the pressure you are under, in an over-crowded prison.

ASST. GOVERNOR. And you think you could do better. I understand.

SILLITOE (*patiently*). Look, I quite appreciate that the last thing you want is Home Office – whizz kids, cluttering up the place with their fancy ideas, I fully understand that. All that's happened is that as a result of one or two – well-publicised, recent cases in which the treatment of similar offenders was considered unsatisfactory . . .

ASST. GOVERNOR. By the popular press.

SILLITOE. By the popular press, yes, and by others, it has been thought that in this case every effort should be made to . . . prevent the same kind of thing happening again.

ASST. GOVERNOR. I see.

SILLITOE. It's all in the letter.

ASST. GOVERNOR. I know.

Slight pause.

SILLITOE (*referring to the report*). Now your chap is quite right, in his way, about her immature personality, psychotic tendencies, that's all absolutely fine, as far as it goes, but he does leave out a number of factors I think are important.

Pause.

ASST. GOVERNOR. Go on.

SILLITOE. Well, one of the things is that it is, in fact, quite normal for people who have severe problems and find it hard to verbalise them, it's quite normal for them to act them out, on the environment, directly, as this girl did, who lost one thing and then took another thing as a substitute. And you see, the only way to get down to this is to make her verbalise, make her face up to herself. And obviously you've found it difficult, quite understandably –

ASST. GOVERNOR. Doctor Sillitoe, what exactly do you want to do?

SILLITOE. For a start, I'd like her off sedation.

ASST. GOVERNOR. Yes. She is already off sedation. And already a great deal more difficult to handle.

SILLITOE. And then I'd like to talk to her.

ASST. GOVERNOR. Yes?

SILLITOE (*patiently*). To find out what happened.

ASST. GOVERNOR. We know what happened, Doctor. She stole a baby for which she was sent to prison.

Pause.

SILLITOE. But you can – you can treat a person, you can treat people as if they were people. You can go that far, surely.

ASST. GOVERNOR. Of course. We do.

She picks up the phone and speaks down it.

Could you have E.J. Millet taken to Room A32 in the hospital wing please. Thank you.

She puts the phone down, stands.

Within the confines of the institution in which we find ourselves.

She puts her chair round the side of the table, and takes the telephone out. SILLITOE *takes out a new packet of cigarettes, opens them, and puts them on the table with a box of matches. Enter the* WARDRESS *with* EILEEN, *looking sullen in her prison clothes.* SILLITOE *stands.*

SILLITOE. Hallo, Eileen.

WARDRESS. Sit down.

> EILEEN *sits untidily at the table.*

When you've finished, please ring the bell, Doctor.

She goes out.

EILEEN *(immediately)*. Right. Get this for starters. No more fucking injections.

SILLITOE. I'm not going to give you any injections Eileen.

EILEEN. I've been walking round in a bloody daze for weeks and I'm not having it no more.

SILLITOE. There's to be no more drugs, I promise. Cigarette?

> EILEEN *shakes her head.*

EILEEN. I won't take 'em. You can't make me.

SILLITOE. Don't worry, Eileen, no-one's going to make you take any more drugs. I just want to talk, see if we can't sort out some of your problems together.

EILEEN. Oh. What d'you want to talk about?

SILLITOE. Well, why don't we start with your childhood, Eileen. Your family.

EILEEN. You know all about that. It's on my file.

SILLITOE. I want you to tell me, in your own words. I can't treat you, you see, till I know you.

> *Spot fades up on* MRS TAYLOR *at the side of the stage. She speaks to the audience.*

MRS TAYLOR. Catherine Taylor. Aged 47. Married, no children. Elder sister of Jane Millet, Eileen's mother.

EILEEN *(shrugs)*. OK.

SILLITOE. Shall we start with your parents?

Pause.

For example, tell me if you ever felt your parents really loved you.

MRS TAYLOR. I think Jane was always disappointed with her husband. Our parents felt that she had married beneath herself, socially, but Jane believed that Maurice would go far. It didn't work out like that. She married a motor mechanic, and she stayed married to a motor mechanic. All their dreams for Maurice's own garage remained just dreams.

EILEEN. Well . . . happen when I were little . . . I mean, I'd nowt else . . .

SILLITOE. But later?

MRS TAYLOR. So I think she transferred a lot of her ambition on to Eileen. She wanted to show the family that her child could make its own way.

EILEEN. Aw, they . . . you know . . .

SILLITOE. I don't know.

EILEEN (aggressively). They muck you about, don't they? Think you're their fucking property.

SILLITOE. And you didn't think that?

EILEEN. Eh?

SILLITOE. That you were their property?

EILEEN. No of course I fucking didn't.

MRS TAYLOR. And of course Eileen didn't live up to Jane's expectations. It wasn't that she was just difficult in the normal way - untidy and moody like all children - she had a vicious streak, she deliberately set out to upset people with her behaviour.

EILEEN. They'd get that angry. Over little things. You know - hair brushing and dirty clothes and that. Even when I were old. They made me go to this college to do domestic science. She had this great vision of me running a restaurant or summat. Domestic fucking Science. I hate cooking. So I got chucked out.

SILLITOE. Why?

EILEEN. Didn't do no work, did I?

MRS TAYLOR. I have no children myself, but I can understand when you've scrimped and saved for an only child, you can become over-ambitious. It's difficult to accept failure, especially unnecessary failure.

SILLITOE. What happened after college?

EILEEN. Oh, I went to work in a carpet factory. Nowt else to do. Got sack there too.

SILLITOE. Why?

EILEEN (*with pleasure*). Well, you see, it were a right good screw, as happened, on night shift, you'd go round back of loom and pull out ends of yarn. And then minder'd have to stop machine and mend 'em. You could work it out, it were one and a half minutes to mend each one. So if you broke half a dozen, you'd have near ten minutes off. Anyroad, they caught me at it.

Pause.

SILLITOE. You told that story with a great deal of – pleasure. Did you find it pleasurable, sabotaging the machine?

EILEEN (*smiling*). It were real.

MRS TAYLOR. I think everybody tried with her. Jane and Maurice weren't perfect parents – who is? But they did their best, according to their lights. It's not their fault, the way Eileen's turned out. They shouldn't be blamed.

Spot on MRS TAYLOR *out, she exits.*

SILLITOE. So you don't really think your parents loved you?

EILEEN. Aw . . . I dunno. They said they did.

SILLITOE. But you didn't believe them.

    EILEEN *shrugs.*

    Did you?

    Pause.

    Tell me, do you think you've ever been loved, like you want to be? By a boyfriend, perhaps?

    Pause. EILEEN *shrugs.*

    Have you had many boyfriends?

EILEEN. Some.

SILLITOE. Have you ever been in love with any of them?

EILEEN. May have.

SILLITOE. I think it would help if I knew.

EILEEN. I don't.

Pause.

SILLITOE. Why not?

Pause.

EILEEN. Don't want to talk about it.

SILLITOE. D'you feel I'm invading your privacy, by asking about it?

EILEEN. Aye, that's what I feel. You're invading my privacy.

SILLITOE. But you're sure that isn't a cover?

EILEEN. A what?

Pause.

SILLITOE (*trying hard*). You see, Eileen, I think you might find it difficult, and this is perfectly understandable, you might find it difficult to talk about your feelings to people.

Pause.

Possibly because you feel guilty about them, your feelings, and because you think people would laugh at you if you told them what they really were.

Pause.

Look, Eileen, you can talk to me. Why not tell me about Shahid.

Pause.

EILEEN. Shahid?

SILLITOE. Yes.

Slight pause.

EILEEN. I love him.

SILLITOE. Why?

EILEEN. What d'you mean, why?

Spot on SHAHID *at the side of the stage.*

SHAHID. Shahid Daz. Aged 22. Born Lahore, in what was West Pakistan. Came to England with family in 1958. Parents returned to Pakistan in 1970. Work in a club. Earn £13.50 a week. Send at least five pounds a week home.

SILLITOE. Tell me what attracted you to him, particularly.

EILEEN. I still don't know what you mean.

SILLITOE. Well, let me put it another way. *(Carefully.)* Did you think about your family at all, when you decided to sleep with Shahid?

EILEEN. What, ooh, if me mam could see me now, me knickers down to a feller?

SILLITOE. No, that's not quite what I meant.

SHAHID. I met Eileen in the club. She looked like death. I thought maybe she was on drugs, she looked like that. But I think she was just very depressed and lonely. So we talked. We became friends. Later, we became – lovers.

SILLITOE. What I mean is, did you – did you think they'd be shocked? Upset?

EILEEN. They'd have gone fucking hairless.

SHAHID. It is too simple to say that Eileen needs to love and needs to be loved. It makes her sound an incomplete person, and we all need love. Eileen found it difficult to achieve because she needed a great intensity of love, and would not compromise.

SILLITOE. Tell me what you think your parents would have said if they'd known.

Slight pause.

EILEEN. Ee, I can hear 'em. It'd have been, ooh, that our Eileen should have sunk so low, after all we've told her, that our Eileen would have so degraded herself, ooh ooh ooh . . .

Pause.

SILLITOE. You liked saying that, didn't you? Making up what your parents would have said?

EILEEN. It's fucking true, I can tell you.

SILLITOE. That you'd degraded yourself? Is that true?

EILEEN. Eh? No, I mean it's true they would have said what I said.

SILLITOE. But isn't it true that you did, in your own eyes, somehow?

EILEEN. I did what?

SILLITOE. Deliberately set out to choose a boyfriend who would, as it were, symbolize rejection of your background and your family?

EILEEN. Eh?

SILLITOE. Didn't you want to degrade yourself, in a way?

EILEEN (*amazed*). Degrade myself?

Slight pause.

SILLITOE. Can I ask you if you'd ever slept with a coloured man before?

EILEEN *looks at* SILLITOE *with contempt, having realised what he was driving at.*

EILEEN. Eh, fuck off.

SHAHID. I think we had what she wanted – and I wanted too – for a moment. And that moment made our child. But things change. You cannot live in isolation.

SILLITOE. Then you are sure you weren't attracted by the mystique, at all? The kind of – mystery attached to someone not from your own country, black or white?

Pause.

Did you imagine, for instance, when you decided to sleep with him, did you think he'd be better than your other lovers, or worse?

Pause.

In bed, that is.

EILEEN (*suddenly, demonstrating the length of a yard with her hands, sarcastic*). And do you know, it were that long.

Pause.

SILLITOE. I can't help you if you won't help me.

SHAHID. The outside world invades the inside world and – things die.

He shrugs. His spot out, and he exits. Pause.

SILLITOE. You don't find it easy, do you, finding good sexual relationships?

EILEEN. Oh, fuck off.

SILLITOE. You like dirty words, don't you.

EILEEN. Eh?

SILLITOE (*checking his notes*). Did you know that since this conversation began you have used the word fuck no less than eight times?

EILEEN. Eh?

SILLITOE. Do you get a kick out of it?

EILEEN. Not half as much as you get talking about me having it off with Pakistanis.

Pause.

SILLITOE. Look, Eileen. What I meant when I talked about degrading, what I was wondering was whether you deliberately degraded yourself, and I don't mean just Shahid, I mean where you lived, no job, etc, etc, but thinking that you'd never find anything better, that sex was all you were good for, that in your own eyes you weren't worth any more. That's what I meant.

Pause.

EILEEN. I remember when my aunty came to see me after I'd – I'd – I'd lost the baby and she kept on about the room, cos it were right tatty, all I could get, and I'm dead sure that if I'd been knocking off some poxy old tramp, in a posh place with clean curtains and central heating, she'd not have minded.

Long pause.

SILLITOE (*very careful*). Have you always liked babies?

EILEEN *shrugs.*

They're very easy to love, aren't they, babies. They don't
answer back. They always need, and give, plenty of affection.

Pause.

Is that why you took Simon?

EILEEN. He weren't called Simon.

SILLITOE. Is that the reason?

Long pause.

EILEEN (*slowly, quietly*). It's bloody real. When I were at school.
They'd say, all the time, being a mother's your role in life,
that's what you're being taught for, the highest and noblest
female duty. And now you say that cos I wanted to be a
mother, cos I wanted a kid, I'm not capable of owt else.
(*Weakly.*) So which am I meant to believe?

SILLITOE. I don't say you're incapable of anything, Eileen.

EILEEN. I don't want to talk any more.

Pause.

SILLITOE. Why was it a boy?

EILEEN. Eh?

SILLITOE. Why did you steal a boy baby?

EILEEN. Does it matter?

SILLITOE. Yes, I think it probably does.

EILEEN (*slight smile*). Do you now?

SILLITOE. Yes.

EILEEN *laughs.*

Why are you laughing?

EILEEN. Let me ask you a question, clever dick. If you were
stealing a baby in a crowded shopping precinct in broad
daylight, would you hang about checking if it had one?

Triumphant pause.

I'd no idea what sex it were, you daft ha'porth.

SILLITOE. Eileen, you're not helping.

EILEEN. Why should I?

SILLITOE. Because if you don't I can't help you to solve your
problems.

EILEEN. Aw, Jesus. Problems. When I was born, I were a
problem. At school I were a problem pupil. At college I were
a problem worker. I thought at least in here I'd just be a
common or garden convict, but no, now I'm a fucking
problem criminal too. Oh, yuh, sure. Sure I'm a fucking
problem *now*.

SILLITOE. What do you mean?

EILEEN. I mean . . . It doesn't matter.

Spot on MRS O'BRIEN *at the side of the stage.*

MRS O'BRIEN. Jacqueline O'Brien. Aged 34. Special Investigator
for the Supplementary Benefits Commission. On the 29th of
February I visited the flat of Eileen Millet, a spinster, aged
20, who was suspected of gaining benefit fraudulently.

SILLITOE. Eileen. It's only by discovering, together, what's
wrong with you, that we can make you better.

Pause.

MRS O'BRIEN. This claimant had been recently dismissed from
her place of work for industrial misconduct, and was
therefore ineligible for unemployment benefit, under Section
22 Subsection Two of the National Insurance Act 1965. She
was, in consequence, receiving supplementary benefit of
£6.25 a week, including rent allowance, having suffered a
reduction of £2.60 on account of her having been dismissed
through her own negligence.

SILLITOE. What you did is evidence that you have terrible
problems, and while no-one claims that prison is the perfect
place to sort them out in, you must accept that we do want to
do our best for you.

Pause.

MRS O'BRIEN. It was noticed that the claimant was pregnant,
and therefore, possibly, cohabiting. My own observations and
interviews with neighbours inclined me to this view. When I
visited her, the claimant admitted that the father of her child

did spend time with her, but denied that he cohabited. I ascertained that his earnings were above the minimum for a couple, and that if cohabiting, therefore, he would be liable to support her.

SILLITOE. And no-one claims that society's methods of dealing with people in trouble are perfect either. But there are people – and I hope I'm one of them – who believe that when problems drive someone into action as extreme as yours, then they should give all the assistance they can. And by assistance I mean sympathy. And understanding. And love.

Pause.

MRS O'BRIEN. I found a pair of men's underpants in the claimant's bedroom, and established that the claimant could provide no alternative address for the young man in question. I therefore expressed to her my view that she was cohabiting, and told her that, under the provisions of the Social Security Act 1966, she was not entitled to benefit. The claimant said that the man in question was unable to support her as he regularly sent a proportion of his wage to Pakistan, but I informed her that this was not a matter for the commission, and that her benefit would accordingly cease forthwith.

Pause.

Three weeks later, the Claimant convinced the Commission that she was no longer cohabiting, and when I had confirmed by investigation that this was indeed the case, her benefit was restored.

MRS O'BRIEN's *spot out and she exits.*

SILLITOE. Eileen, do you feel guilt?

EILEEN. Guilt?

SILLITOE. At what you did.

EILEEN. You want me to feel guilty?

SILLITOE. No, I don't *want* you to feel guilty. I think you *do* feel guilty.

EILEEN. In't that same thing?

SILLITOE. No it isn't, Eileen.

Pause.

Do you ever feel that what you do is right or wrong?

Pause.

Do you ever use those words to yourself?

Pause.

Did you think of right and wrong when you took the baby?

Long pause.

EILEEN. Of course not. You know what happened. I – took him – because I thought he was mine.

SILLITOE (*carefully*). And then you realised he wasn't yours . . .

EILEEN. Yes.

SILLITOE. . . . he was somebody else's, and then did you feel –

EILEEN. No, he wasn't!

SILLITOE. What?

EILEEN. He wasn't somebody else's.

SILLITOE. He wasn't yours, Eileen, you said so.

EILEEN. He wasn't anybody's.

Suddenly angry.

He wasn't anybody's.

Stands, half-hysterical, bangs table.

He wasn't fucking anybody's! That's whole fucking thing!

EILEEN *remains standing, quivering with anger.* SILLITOE *stands, goes round to her.*

SILLITOE. Now come on, Eileen. Keep calm. If you don't keep calm, I can't help you –

EILEEN. Help me?

SILLITOE. Yes, Eileen.

EILEEN. Help me 'solve my problems'.

SILLITOE. Help you to get better.

EILEEN. And what does better mean? Me going out of here and not doing it again?

SILLITOE. Well, partly, of course, but –

EILEEN. Well, go on, then. Check if it's worked.

She sits.

Show me a baby and see if I pinch it.

Pause.

SILLITOE. All right, Eileen. I think that might as well be it for now. I'll have you taken back to your cell. (*He's moving to press the bellpush when* EILEEN *speaks.*)

EILEEN. You're not first, you know.

SILLITOE. What?

EILEEN. They sent a priest in first. Cos I'm Catholic. He said I were a sinner and that Christ says you should treat sinners with compassion. And I said, what's compassion. And he said, love. But he meant pity.

Pause. Direct to SILLITOE.

And now you come with same, only different words.

SILLITOE *goes round and sits in his chair.*

SILLITOE. What do you mean by that?

EILEEN (*getting angry*). I mean that he said I were a sinner and offered me compassion to make me good; you say I'm mental –

SILLITOE. No, I –

EILEEN (*stands*). You say I'm mental and offer me 'help' to make me sane. And neither's looking at me. He's looking at a sin and you're looking at a fucking problem.

Pause.

Well?

SILLITOE *has given up. He doesn't reply.*

Ooh, I may deserve all I've got. I may deserve locking up for ever. But I'm not that bad. I'm not bad enough to deserve your help.

Pause. SILLITOE *presses the bellpush.*

SILLITOE. Sit down, Eileen.

EILEEN *remains standing. Enter* WARDRESS *and* 2nd WARDRESS.

Eileen can go back to her cell now.

2nd WARDRESS *goes to* EILEEN, *takes her arm.* EILEEN *goes rigid, refuses to move.*

2nd WARDRESS. Come on, Millet. Don't be silly.

EILEEN *gives up, shakes her head, and allows the* WARDRESS *to lead her out. The* ASSISTANT GOVERNOR *appears.*

ASST. GOVERNOR. Well?

SILLITOE. Worth a try.

ASST. GOVERNOR. And now?

SILLITOE. We'll put her back on largactil. I'll review the case in a week. Have another bash.

ASST. GOVERNOR. Right. Thank you, doctor.

She goes out quickly. A long pause. SILLITOE *follows the* ASSISTANT GOVERNOR *out. The* WARDRESSES *wheel in* EILEEN, *under a blanket, on a trolley. They go out again. Then they return, the* WARDRESS *with a hypodermic syringe in an enamel tray, and the* 2nd WARDRESS *with a swab and other injection equipment. They stand either side of the trolley.* EILEEN *notices them vaguely.*

2nd WARDRESS. There you are.

WARDRESS. Where've you been?

EILEEN *smiles vaguely, as the* WARDRESSES *put their equipment on the trolley.*

2nd WARDRESS. Just woken up, have you?

Pause.

Come on, then, up you come.

WARDRESS *and* 2nd WARDRESS *help* EILEEN *into a sitting position.* WARDRESS *takes* EILEEN's *arm as:*

We're back now.

WARDRESS (*rolling up* EILEEN's *sleeve*). That's right.

EILEEN *is aware of what's happening to her arm, slight look of panic.*

2nd WARDRESS (*quickly, to divert* EILEEN's *attention, but gently*). Hey, you want a hug, don't you?

EILEEN *looks at* 2nd WARDRESS.

WARDRESS (*filling the hypodermic*). Course you do.

2nd WARDRESS. You want a cuddle.

2nd WARDRESS *cuddles* EILEEN *to keep her from looking at the* WARDRESS *who is swabbing* EILEEN's *arm.*

Who's a daft one, then?

WARDRESS. Our little baby.

WARDRESS *gives* EILEEN *the injection.* EILEEN *stiffens.*

2nd WARDRESS (*holding* EILEEN *tight*). No crying now. No.

WARDRESS *lays* EILEEN's *arm down and holds* EILEEN *to lower her back on to the trolley.*

Our little baby, cos you love us, eh?

WARDRESS *and* 2nd WARDRESS *start to lower* EILEEN *gently down on to the trolley.*

WARDRESS. So much, eh?

EILEEN *is down. The lights begin to fade, and we hear the church music from the beginning of the play, softly.*

2nd WARDRESS. We love you so much.

EILEEN (*very nearly asleep*). Yes. Yes. Yes.

The music grows louder as the stage fades to blackout.

End of play.

THE NATIONAL THEATRE

Characters

ELLA – late 20s.
MARIE – mid 20s.
CHUB – about 30.
EILEEN – about 20.
ALEX – mid 30s.

Notes

The action of most of the play takes place during the broadcast of
Radio Four's 'The World at One'. This broadcast is not
continuous. Ideally, the programme should be recorded on the
day of performance, so that, if the play is performed at lunchtime,
we are hearing what happened ten or fifteen minutes before the
performance began. An alternative is to use the pre-recorded
programme of the day before. The aim of this device is to provide
a random element in each individual performance.

The speech at the end of the play was delivered by Harold Wilson
in the summer of 1975. It could be any speech, by any
Government politician, at more or less any time.

The National Theatre was first presented at the Open Space Theatre,
London, in October 1975. The cast was as follows:

ELLA	Katharine Schofield
MARIE	Lynda Marchal
CHUB	Brian Gwaspari
EILEEN	Lindsay Ingram
ALEX	Robert Oates

Directed by Peter Stevenson
Designed by Vivienne Cartwright

ACT ONE

Lights on a dressing-room. A screen. Two mirrors at tables, one cracked. On the uncracked mirror, someone has written EILEEN *in make-up. A third mirror is propped up against the back of a chair, over which hangs a quilted nylon dressing gown.*

A day-bed, on it, one or two glossy sex magazines.

ELLA *enters. She is in her late 20s, middle-class, wearing faded blue-jeans and a printed tee-shirt, possibly advertising a West End show. She has a bag, which she puts on the table in front of the cracked mirror. Then she sits, facing the audience.*

Then she concentrates, as if preparing herself for something. Then she starts to speak.

ELLA. 'It's a year to the day since father died. This very day, May the Fifth, Irena's saint's day. It was very cold, and snowing, I remember, and I thought that I could not survive his death; and you had fainted and were lying still, so still we thought you dead. And now – a year has passed, we talk of it so easily. You're dressed in white, look, and your face is shining, radiant . . .'

She looks round, sees a metal ashtray, picks it up, bangs it on the table twelve times.

'The clock struck twelve then, too.'

She stands and moves during:

'I remember when father was being driven to the graveyard, there was a military band, and a salute with rifle fire, because he was a general, in charge of a brigade. But there weren't that many people there. Although, of course, it rained that day. Rained hard, and snowed as well.'

Delivering the line, from another character, flatly, as a cue.

'Need we bring up all these memories.'

Sits, back to performance.

'Today it's warm. We can have the windows open, yet there's no leaves showing on the birch trees. Father was made a

Brigadier eleven years ago, and then he moved from
Moscow, took us with him. I remember well how everything
in Moscow was in blossom now, everything was drenched in
warmth and sunlight.'

Enter MARIE, *mid-20s, slight regional accent, dressed uncaringly in a
dress, carrying a supermarket carrier-bag. She stands, watches* ELLA,
*who doesn't notice her. After a moment or two, she takes a radio from
the carrier-bag, and puts it on one of the tables.* ELLA *continues.*

ELLA. 'Eleven years! Yet I remember everything as if we'd left
there yesterday. Oh, heaven! When I woke this morning, saw
this flood of sun, this springtime sun, I felt so moved and
happy! Such a longing to go back, back home to Moscow!'

MARIE *turns the radio on.* BLEEP BLEEP BLEEP BLEEP BLEEP
BLEEP BLEEEEEP. *Then the beginning of the Radio Four lunchtime
news programme 'The World At One'.* ELLA *looks up at* MARIE.
MARIE *gives a slight smile.* ELLA *goes to the cracked mirror, takes a
kimono dressing gown from her bag, puts it over the back of the chair,
takes off her tee-shirt, sits, starts making up. The radio goes on.*
MARIE *goes to the uncracked mirror, takes a Kleenex, rubs out*
EILEEN, *writes up* MARIE. *Then she goes and takes the nylon
dressing gown, hangs it over the chair in front of her new mirror. She
takes off her dress, and sits, in her underwear, looking at herself. She
feels her breasts, inspecting them.* ELLA *looks at her.* MARIE *smiles
back, turns up the radio slightly.* ELLA *looks at the radio. This little
self-conscious pantomime carries on a few moments.*

MARIE. I like to keep abreast of events.

ELLA. Ah.

MARIE. The unfolding of the sacred drama of our times.

ELLA. Of course.

Pause.

The sacred drama. Yes.

MARIE. Did you know, in Germany, in the 20's, a guy left a
suitcase full of money, in a train compartment, went to have
a piss. Got back, and found the suitcase stolen. But they'd
left the cash.

ELLA. No, no, I hadn't known that.

MARIE. What we're heading for. Apparently.

Pause. MARIE *raises her arms. Shrugs, finds a battery razor in her carrier-bag.* ELLA *offers* MARIE *a cigarette.*

ELLA. D'you want a fag?

MARIE. No thanks, I've given up.

ELLA. Well done.

MARIE *starts shaving her armpits. The radio statics.* ELLA *lights her cigarette.*

I really resent shaving.

MARIE. Mm?

ELLA. One would have thought the good God would have spared us that, at least. Having given us so much else to put up with.

MARIE. Don't do it, then.

MARIE *finishes shaving.*

ELLA (*half-shrug*). The feminine mystique.

MARIE. Oh, yes.

Pause. MARIE *stands, energetically, goes to the day-bed, lies down, picks up a glossy, looks through it.*

ELLA. I once went out with a bloke whose ideal woman didn't sweat, excrete or menstruate. So instead of saying I had the curse when I really meant I didn't want it, I had to say I didn't want it, when I really meant I had the curse.

MARIE. Why did you bother?

ELLA. I was very much in love. Love is – putting up with his Madonna complex.

MARIE (*stands*). Love is – never having to say you're soggy.

ELLA *smiles. Pause.*

Where's little 'leen?

ELLA *shrugs.*

Mm.

MARIE *picks up her dressing gown, puts it on, and exits.* ELLA *turns off the radio, looks at herself in the mirror. Then turns to where* MARIE *has gone.*

ELLA. 'O, Masha, do stop whistling! How can you?'

Turns back.

'I suppose I must get these constant headaches because I have to go to school each day and go on teaching right into the evening. I seem to think like someone quite old. In fact, in fact –'

Re-enter MARIE, who goes to her table, turns on the radio, takes a toilet roll from her carrier-bag, as.

MARIE. Little girl's room's paperless again.

Exit MARIE. ELLA switches off the radio. Pause.

ELLA. 'In fact, I feel my energy and youth, just dripping out of me, drop by drop, day after day, for these four years that I've been . . . just . . .'

Pause. Groping for the line.

'I've just . . .'

Quickly, a remembered rather than a delivered line.

'One longing and it grows and grows . . .'

She stands.

'I can't help thinking that if I had married, stayed at home, it would have been, I would have been . . .'

Pause. Remembering the line, but this time delivering it.

'I would have been so fond of him, my husband.'

Pause.

Ridiculous.

She sits. Shrugs, puts on the radio. Takes a take-away sandwich from her bag and eats. Enter CHUB, a youngish, slightly vacuous man, dressed in blue denim. ELLA looks round, sees him. She stands, puts on her kimono, sits, carries on eating.

CHUB. Eileen?

ELLA. Don't know.

CHUB. Marie?

ELLA. John.

CHUB. Eh?

ELLA. Toilet.

CHUB. Ah. Eileen?

ELLA. I don't know, Chub.

CHUB. The Colonel likes people here in good time.

Pause. CHUB *takes out a quarter-bottle of whisky.*

Drink?

ELLA *shakes her head.*

Never before a show, eh.

Pause.

Professional.

ELLA. That's right.

CHUB (*sits on the day-bed, turns the pages of the glossy* MARIE *left there*). Are you nervous? I mean, do you get nervous? Flutterbyes in the tummy, sinking feeling, first night nerves?

Pause.

First lunch nerves, I should say.

ELLA. I want to change now, Chub.

CHUB. I'm always petrified. Even in my lowly capacity. No reason. Silly, isn't it.

Slight pause.

So I need my little drink.

ELLA. OK?

CHUB (*stands*). You shouldn't eat. Before you perform. Get cramp.

Enter MARIE *with her toilet roll.*

ELLA. All right?

CHUB. Eileen should be here by now, you know.

MARIE. Hello, Chub.

CHUB. Hello, Marie.

MARIE. Piss off, Chub. Ella wants to change.

She goes and sits. CHUB, *after a moment, shrugs and exits.* MARIE *turns the radio down, to a murmur.*

It must be your dulcet middle-class tones.

ELLA. Eh?

MARIE. The attraction. Why he buzzes round you like a vulture at the Alamo.

ELLA. Eh?

MARIE. He has this desire to dominate his social superiors.

Slight pause.

It's a great mystery, of course, the root of his resentment at the genteel classes. Perhaps he was bitten by one as a child.

Slight pause.

Can I have a bite?

ELLA. Sure.

MARIE *takes a bite from* ELLA's *roll. Speaks with her mouth full.*

MARIE. I gather the only fantasy that's guaranteed to get Chub's plums off is the trussing up and subsequent mild flagellation of Esther Rantzen.

ELLA. Urgh.

During the following, MARIE *brushes her hair and then plaits it.*

I'm not really middle-class.

MARIE. No?

ELLA. Not really.

MARIE. Insult, i'n'it. Bourgeois respectability. The working-class wears overalls all day and puts on suits at night. The middle-class wears suits all day and dresses up in denim to go out. What a world we live in.

ELLA (*stops work for a moment*). Would that I were.

MARIE. Bourgeois?

ELLA. Respectable.

MARIE. You don't mean that.

ELLA. I don't?

MARIE. You mean you wish you were respected. Not the same at all.

ELLA. Do you?

MARIE. I'm perfectly delighted with my life. To date. Thank you. I'm in complete control.

Enter EILEEN. *She is 20, cockney, fashionable and neatly dressed.*

EILEEN (*sings, well-meaning but uncertain*). Another opening, another show –

ELLA. Eileen.

MARIE. Hi, 'leen.

EILEEN (*notices where* MARIE *is sitting*). Hey, that's my –

MARIE. No it isn't.

EILEEN. Put my name up.

MARIE. Tough.

EILEEN. That's my personal mirror.

MARIE. It has just been liberated.

She gestures towards the third mirror. Then, during the following, her hair down, she stands to lean further into the mirror to make up her eyes:

EILEEN. Sod you.

MARIE. Turf or buggery?

EILEEN. You what?

MARIE turns the radio up. EILEEN *crossly empties her make-up out of her bag on to the chair with the propped-up mirror. She goes behind the screen, returns with a coat-hanger. She hangs up her jacket. She is about to take off her jumper when, for some reason, she thinks better of it. She looks round at the others, half-guilty.* MARIE *still concentrating on her eyes.* ELLA *has begun to pull faces in the mirror, obviously some exercise. She will continue to do this for some time.* EILEEN *tries to look in the mirror. Too low. She looks round, sees* MARIE *is not sitting, takes her chair and sits. But, even sitting, she finds it uncomfortable. So she stands, returns the chair, is going back to her mirror as* MARIE *sits down again.* EILEEN *turns back, annoyed that* MARIE *has apparently not noticed the chair's absence. Then* EILEEN *kneels in front of the chair and starts to make up.*

MARIE. You'll get it all smudged.

EILEEN. Pardon?

MARIE. If you keep your jumper on. When you take it off, you'll smudge your make-up.

EILEEN. 's all right.

MARIE. Well, it isn't. You'll go on with a smudgy face. And then what will your public think.

EILEEN. Oh, bugger off.

MARIE *(turns)*. Now, that's specific. Vulgar, indicative of linguistic starvation at an early age, but at least refreshingly free of ambiguity.

EILEEN *doesn't reply.* MARIE *turns back.*

Many in?

EILEEN. Many what?

MARIE. Punters.

EILEEN. Dunno.

Pause. MARIE *turns down the radio.*

MARIE. A sunny day. Lunch in Hyde Park. Fatten the ducks. And instead they come, to sit in a sweaty shoebox, watching us. Now why?

EILEEN. Why what?

MARIE. Why do they come.

EILEEN. *So* they can come, I suppose.

MARIE *turns.* EILEEN *grins. Explaining.*

Fantasies. Frustrated.

MARIE *(turns back)*. Bored. Ella, what the fuck are you doing?

For the last few moments, ELLA *has been vibrating her lips with her fingers.*

ELLA (*stops, embarrassed*). Um –

MARIE (*imitates*). Dubberdubberdubber . . .

EILEEN (*stands, pleased*). What you doing, Ella?

MARIE. Dubberdubberdubber . . .

ELLA. It's an exercise.

MARIE. Exercise? What for?

EILEEN. Eh, you learn that at Radar, Ella?

ELLA. RADA, not Radar.

MARIE. What's it for, Ella?

> *Slight pause.*

ELLA. It's for my voice. It releases the muscles of the lips.
Relaxes the vocal chords.

EILEEN. But you don't say anything.

ELLA. No, but –

> MARIE *stands, takes black stockings, suspender belt, navy-blue
> underwear from her carrier-bag and changes into them, as:*

MARIE. Ah, but she does. You forget the backchat, little 'leen.

EILEEN. Oh, yuh.

MARIE. Oh my word yes. The quick responses and the repartee.
Must have her chords relaxed to blind them with her razor-
sharp rejoinders. Her sophisticated little quips and
sophistries.

EILEEN. Classy.

MARIE. Absolutely. Breeding. Savoir faire. Born not made. More
than a touch of arse.

> *Pause.* MARIE *waiting for a response.*

ELLA (*not looking at* MARIE). To what do I owe the pleasure, dear
Marie? Got out of the wrong bed this morning?

> *Slight pause. Then* MARIE *behind the screen, puts her costume on, as
> she continues.*

MARIE. Particularly today. World premiere. Everybody here. The foyer thronged with gay first nighters. The atmosphere but thick with Hormone slap-on after-shower'n'shave. The air alive with rattling Krugerrands. See here, a social columnist, checking the crowds for dangereuses liaisons. See there, a critic, sharpening his pencil and an apposite bon mot. And there again, a covey, charm or chattering of West End impressarios, their cheque books poised, and there again –

ELLA. Shut up, Marie.

MARIE. Offensive? Near the knuckle? Opening old sores?

ELLA. No. Boring.

MARIE *appears in a schoolgirl costume, hat, white shirt, tie, gymslip, carrying a satchel and a lolly.*

MARIE. Right. Proppies. See our little lolly and our satchel's set.

Exit MARIE. EILEEN *chuckles.* ELLA *looks at her.*

EILEEN. She's very funny.

ELLA. Yes.

EILEEN. I'm sorry.

ELLA. Why does she get like that? So suddenly.

EILEEN *(returns to finish her make-up).* How should I know? P'raps she's jealous.

ELLA. Jealous?

EILEEN. Of your past.

ELLA. I'm jealous of her future.

Pause.

Better change.

Slight pause.

She's right, you know. You'll smudge your face.

ELLA *goes behind the screen.*

EILEEN. Um, Ella –

ELLA. Yes?

EILEEN. Ella, I got a problem.

ELLA *reappears, carrying, on a hanger, a short-skirted and too-small WRAF uniform, again with black stockings, suspenders and brief black underwear.*

ELLA. Yes?

Slight pause.

EILEEN. Nothing.

ELLA (*undressing*). I can play the piano. Rather well. I can communicate, as if in my living room, with the back row of the circle at Drury Lane. I can do a passable cockney, Lancs, Black Country and South Yorkshire. I can do an adequate Scottish, Irish, Devon and Scouse. My Welsh is erratic and my Geordie is embarrassing but I do a pretty good Southern States though over a long evening it does have a tendency to travel. I can speak French and Spanish and a smattering of German. It has sometimes struck me that in the context of my present employment I could be seen as somewhat over-qualified. My credentials something of an unnecessary luxury.

ELLA *suddenly turns up the radio, retunes to a pop programme, and dresses, as a reverse-strip, to the music. As she does so, EILEEN takes off her jumper. It's painful. She smudges her make-up. EILEEN's front and back are covered with cuts and bruises. When she's dressed, ELLA turns off the radio.*

There will now be a short emission.

She goes to the table and sits. Quotes, half to herself.

In fact, not even a luxury . . . A useless encumbrance . . . like having six fingers on your hand.

She counts her fingers.

Well, that's a relief.

To EILEEN, but not looking at her.

You better change.

EILEEN. Ella.

ELLA. Yes?

EILEEN. I got a problem.

ELLA. Yes?

EILEEN. 'Bout going on today.

ELLA. Yes?

EILEEN. Look at me.

> ELLA *looks at* EILEEN.

ELLA. Oh, blimey.

EILEEN. I put some stuff on, but it's just bringing 'em out.

ELLA. You should have said.

EILEEN. When?

ELLA. Earlier.

> *Pause.* EILEEN *looks away.*

> I see. You couldn't. Not in front of madam. Not expose your tender places to her biting edge.

EILEEN *(shrugs)*. OK, forget it.

ELLA *(stands)*. Come on, lovely. Let's try a cover-up.

EILEEN *(stands)*. They'll come out a treat under the U/V.

ELLA. At the moment, they'd come out a treat in the dark. Lie down. Tummy up.

> EILEEN *lies down, on her back, on the day-bed.* ELLA *takes a tin of powder, and during the following, tries to cover* EILEEN's *bruises.*

EILEEN. Thanks, Ella.

ELLA. You're a right old mess.

EILEEN. Yuh, am.

ELLA. Can I ask how –

EILEEN. Well, I didn't get 'em falling down the stairs.

ELLA. No.

> *Slight pause.*

> Have you told the police?

EILEEN. Well, I can't really. Can I.

ELLA. Why not?

EILEEN. It's my husband.

Pause.

ELLA. Oh. I didn't realise. I thought it was a mugger, or a . . . You know.

EILEEN. Yuh.

ELLA *still powdering* EILEEN's *bruises.*

You can't, you see, there's no such thing, in legal terms, as your husband raping you. You can't get done, for, as it were, rolling your own.

Pause.

It's funny, 'cos he usually, he doesn't like it much. Gets a bigger rise out of his Alfa, than he does from me.

ELLA. Why did he do it, then?

EILEEN (*shrugs*). Punishment.

ELLA. For what?

Pause.

EILEEN. He knows we need the money.

Slight pause.

ELLA. Right. Turn over.

EILEEN (*does so*). I wouldn't mind, but I got this audition.

ELLA. What for?

EILEEN. Telly. Dancing, with a group of dancers on the telly.

ELLA. When?

EILEEN. Would you believe, 5pm?

ELLA. Today?

EILEEN. Today. Don't think he wanted me to get it.

ELLA. Why?

EILEEN. 'Cos his rich chums aren't likely to see me cavorting about here. Or if they do, they're hardly going to mention it.

Slight pause.

Don't you want to? Get another job?

ELLA. I s'pose I need to think I do.

ELLA looks away. Pause. EILEEN notices the open sexmag, where CHUB left it, near her, on the floor.

EILEEN. 'It wasn't predictable, you understand. He was just standing there, and he said he wanted me. And I laughed, I mean I thought it was a joke, because we'd had this frightful row. Until I saw the bulge in his trousers, and then, without a word, quite suddenly, he hit me, right across the breasts, and shouting, "Don't you laugh at me, you bitch", he kept on hitting me, I struggled with him, but it wasn't any good, he grabbed my shoulders, roughly forced me down on to the kitchen table',

ELLA turns to EILEEN, surprised.

'then and there, and held me down with one hand, while he pushed the other up my skirt and started feeling for my bush, beneath my panties, and we both knew at an instant I was wet and really wanted it my slit was pulsing with desire and when he touched my –'

EILEEN turns the page of the sexmag. ELLA realises EILEEN is reading.

'Angela. Executive's Girl Friday. Merseyside'.

ELLA takes the magazine.

ELLA. They can't be real.

EILEEN. No. Fantasies.

Pause. ELLA shuts the magazine. Quite brightly.

ELLA. It may well be, of course, that Sigmund got it wrong. That dirty pictures, masturbation, driving Alfas aren't, in fact, just pale and insufficient substitutes for sex, but that sex is just a pale and insufficient substitute for Alfas, porn and masturbation. Mm?

She opens the magazine again, looks at it.

We all need fantasies. Until the world fills up the gap, between what we have and what we feel we need. Deserve. Our fantasies, cosmetic, so our lives can live with their reflection in the glass.

Pause. She puts the magazine down.

You poor old thing.

EILEEN. He said he's going to throw me out. Said, on his own, he wouldn't need the money. Said he didn't need a slut to live off any more.

ELLA. Shh. Shh. You poor old thing.

Long pause. ELLA *very gently powders* EILEEN's *skin. Enter* MARIE.

MARIE. Ah. A little relaxatory massage?

ELLA (*stands*). OK, let's have a look.

EILEEN *stands. The bruises still showing through.*

MARIE. Oh, bloody hell. What a mess.

ELLA. Yes, isn't she.

MARIE. How d'you get those then, 'leen?

ELLA. Her husband beat her up.

MARIE. Why?

EILEEN. Not working is it.

ELLA. No. Look, there's some stuff, Passavonate, it's quite pricey, but it should make a better . . . any chemist should have –

EILEEN. I'll nip out then.

EILEEN *quickly dresses as:*

MARIE. Why?

ELLA. Drop it, Marie.

MARIE. Well, I only –

ELLA. You'd better hurry.

MARIE. Couldn't she send Chub?

EILEEN. Oh, do us a favour.

EILEEN *looks at her watch, she's dressed.*

Won't take a minute.

Exit EILEEN. MARIE *to her table, switches on the radio, realises it's pop, retunes to Radio Four. A pause.*

MARIE. Well, poor old 'leen.

ELLA. She ought to get out of it.

MARIE. What?

ELLA. This.

MARIE. Why?

ELLA. Because that's why he beats her up.

MARIE. Then she ought to get out of him.

ELLA. That's absurd.

MARIE. No it's not. She doesn't get beaten up here, in the sink of iniquity. She gets beaten up behind closed curtains in a villa-type residence in Twickenham.

Pause.

She went off it, peeling, when they married, hubby being somewhat bourgeoisly respectable, though not, I'd think, respected. But his aspirations rather overtook his income, with particular regard to Twickers villas, not to mention flashy cars, and so dear Eileen potters back up West to supplement his growing appetites, and p'raps she's only got herself to blame.

ELLA. That's very hard.

MARIE. That doesn't stop it being true.

Suddenly, MARIE switches off the radio, and, in mime, strips herself across the room, singing a blousy tune. During this ELLA sits. At the door, MARIE meets ALEX entering. ALEX is in his mid-30s, wears a suit. MARIE salutes him.

MARIE. Hallo, Colonel.

ALEX. 'Ease.

He kisses MARIE.

Everyone ready?

ELLA. Everyone ready.

ALEX. That's good. It's a nice day. Lots of people on the streets. Attracted by our cool doorway.

MARIE. Yuh.

Pause.

ALEX. You're both looking delightful. All my girls look good, we aren't a slutty joint, we don't employ slags or tarts, but you two are, especially. Delightful.

ELLA. Thanks, Colonel.

ALEX. Where's Eileen?

Pause.

Where's Eileen?

MARIE. In the john.

ALEX. She's ready?

MARIE. Yes.

ALEX. That's good. It's vital to achieve – a frame of mind.

Pause.

I had some notes to give. Just a couple of things I wanted to remind you of. Perhaps, Marie, you'd give Eileen a replay.

MARIE. Sure.

ALEX. Just two or three, small things.

He sits, takes out a notebook.

Right. One. Don't forget, the moment that you're on, you're on. Entrances and exits. We don't want some harlot slopping on and then, the number starts and suddenly she's Tiger Lil. First sighting, vitally important, 'cos then the punter knows, whether he's interested in what's beneath. You buy them then, you'll sell them anything.

He looks up at MARIE. MARIE *smiles.*

Two. Do remember, all of us have got our strong and weak points. Emphasise the former. Push your capabilities. Some of you have got good tits, and others are rather better in the derriere department. Give them most of what you've got the best of. Play on strengths.

Slight pause.

Three. Careful of the eyes. Throughout, but especially when you're on the floor, remember what you're doing, in effect, is making love. And not just with some abstract figure, you are making love with every member of the audience. Passionately and personally. That's what they've paid their money for, to watch themselves make love. And you can clench your bum and flop your bristols all you like, it's not worth a nun's fanny if they look up and see a dead-eyed face considering its lunch. So. Eyes.

Slight pause.

And four, by the same token, watch getting internal in the doubles. If you get something going that's amusing, gets across, that's fine. But no in-jokes or backchat. They haven't come to watch a private conversation. You may be feeling up each other, but you're not dykes. You're merely waiting for the right man, the only man who'll satisfy your lustful appetites. And who is he? He's Mr Punter. Each and every Mr P's the superprick that you are aching for. All right?

MARIE. All right.

ALEX. That's good.

He glances at his watch.

She's in the toilet?

MARIE. Yuh.

Slight pause. MARIE *goes and sits on a chair, the wrong way round, near* ALEX.

MARIE. Hey, are there many in?

ALEX. Oh, yes.

During the following, he and MARIE *touch each other, gently, affectionately.*

Tourists. Hot from the Changing of the Guard. Keen to see England swing. Then on to the Tower and the Planetarium before an evening at the Aldwych. A balanced day.

Slight pause.

You know, now, entertainment is our major national asset. Entertainment, culture, now, the only thing we're still thought best at.

Slight pause.

So, my sweetling, you are, in your own way, Backing Britain.

MARIE. Relieving pressure, on the pound.

ALEX. Boosting reserves.

MARIE. All those lovely dollars, marks and krona.

ALEX. And, on the evidence of the door, yen.

Pause. He looks at ELLA, *looks back at* MARIE, *smiles.* MARIE *smiles.*

MARIE. It's a bloody good show.

ALEX. Yes.

Pause.

I often wonder if I could have made a career in the legitimate theatre. Sometimes I'm disgusted by my work, but when I find myself working with such charming people, and, in addition, helping my country, then I feel quite proud. And what we are doing, in a very simple, unpretentious, unhypocritical way, is giving people what they want, escape from all the rotten news, a little yard of sun in all the gloom. I don't think that escapism's a bad word, as they'd have us think. And when you're working, you are working with an audience, together, you're giving them yourselves, in a co-operative fashion. You're not shoving a message down their throats, you're not trying to shock or frighten them. I often feel, if we could all work together, I mean the country as a whole, if all sides of industry, the government, the people, could all work together as we work together, with each other, and our public, happy in our work, then we'd not have this mess, this trough of idleness and misery. That's my view, anyway.

Pause.

I shall buy you all lunch after the show.

ELLA. Thanks, Colonel.

MARIE *kisses* ALEX.

ALEX. My name's Alex. I don't know why you call me Colonel.

ELLA (*gently, smiling*). Joke.

EILEEN *enters.*

EILEEN. I got the – oh.

ALL *look at her. Pause.* ALEX *stands.*

ALEX. I thought you were ready. We start in seven minutes. You're not ready. Your make-up's smudged. Where the fuck have you been. You look like a slut. Get your sodding frock on.

He goes behind the screen, fetches a baby-doll nightie costume, nightie, white knickers, white ankle-socks, thrusts it at EILEEN.

Now.

EILEEN *begins to change.* ALEX *sees her bruises.*

What's this?

EILEEN *still. To* MARIE.

I blame you for this. You lied to me. You used your position in my life to lie to me.

He looks at EILEEN.

Oh, Mother.

ELLA. Alex, you're a cunt.

ALEX. Say that again!

ELLA. A cunt.

ALEX. That's lovely, Ella. Beautiful.

Exit ALEX, *quickly.* EILEEN *finishes changing, sits.*

ELLA. Why don't you leave that shit, Marie.

MARIE. Why don't you leave that shit, Eileen.

ELLA. Why don't you leave that shit, Marie.

Slight pause.

MARIE. We're not that close. And, I'm a shit too, I suppose. We are shits that pass in the night –

ELLA. Oh, for Christ's sake, Marie –

EILEEN *stands, quickly. This dialogue fast:*

EILEEN. I wouldn't mind, but I got this audition. They're bound to want to see my legs.

MARIE. Audition? What for?

EILEEN (*goes behind screen*). Television. Dancing.

MARIE. Where's the difference?

EILEEN. Well, at least it's –

MARIE (*sings*). Something better than this . . .

> EILEEN *reappears, clutching a big white teddy bear.*

EILEEN. Eh?

MARIE. Sweet Charity. Movie. Shirley Maclaine as a tart with a heart of pure gilt.

> EILEEN *looks at* MARIE *for a second, then starts going through her act. She mimes undressing, using the teddy-bear, going through the little tableaux, pouting, beckoning and so on, then into various poses, some standing, some on the floor.*

EILEEN. ONE two three. ONE two three . . .

ELLA. Why are you so vicious. Her and me.

MARIE. You make me sick. Your guilt.

ELLA. You make you sick. Your guilt.

MARIE. I don't. You may. I know what you're implying. But I DON'T.

> MARIE *goes and switches the radio on, loud.*

ELLA. Oh, switch that bloody thing off.

MARIE. There's nothing wrong with my life. I'm perfectly delighted with my life.

ELLA. Your life, our life, is utterly degrading, tawdry, hypocritical. Admit that, at least. Live with it.

EILEEN (*still rehearsing*). ONE two three, ONE two . . .

MARIE. There's nothing tawdry about my life, I'm in complete control.

ELLA. A lie. A fiction. Just bit parts in other people's masturbation fantasies.

EILEEN (*makes a mistake*). Sod. ONE two three . . .

MARIE. A not ignoble calling.

ELLA (*goes to her*, MARIE *looking firmly away, into the mirror*). Oh, yes. And you're very good, Marie. The Colonel told me. Said you were his number one. Top of the Jerktar rating, you, he said –

EILEEN. ONE two –

MARIE (*switches off the radio, turns*). That's not a –

ELLA. Going to go a long way. Going to be a stripastar. A peelaqueen. Going to put Linda Lovelace in the shade, he said, the newest, nudest –

EILEEN. ONE two three –

> MARIE *switches the radio on, very loud, turns it off, holds it up.*
> EILEEN *still.*

MARIE. The national masturbation fantasy. The nation, observing its own intercourse. The scabby. Crabby. Poxy. Body Politic.

Pause. EILEEN *looks up.*

I tell, no more lies. I'm no more, deceitful, meaningless or cruel . . . than what is daily said . . .

Slight pause.

And, you know, believing that underneath my knickers is my bum is, by the laws of probability, a damn sight safer bet than crediting that underneath those solemn calls for sacrifice, the holy phrases, national interest, Britain First, the Spirit of Dunkirk and keep your straight bat burning, that beneath that there is anything beyond – a vicious, undiminished, and old-fashioned, urge, and need, to screw. In every sense. To screw.

ELLA. So?

MARIE. I'd prefer, in fact, the Peephole, or the Vie Parisienne, or Bottoms Up. I would prefer the centre-fold of Wank or Spank or Slit or Clit. I'd take The French Correction, My Bare Lady, Casanova Goes Kung Fu or Swinging Swedish Exorcists. I'd have all that –

ELLA. Ta-ra-ra-boomdiay!

MARIE. What.

ELLA. The French Correction. Now, that's frightfully good.

MARIE. What?

ELLA. Casanova goes Kung Fu. That's awfully clever.

MARIE. At least –

ELLA. Is there really a magazine called Clit?

MARIE. At least there's something underneath.

EILEEN (*starts again*). ONE two three ONE two three . . .

MARIE. Appealing. Sunny. Warm. And beautiful, perhaps. OK?

ELLA (*sits*). I'm getting out.

MARIE. Now?

ELLA. No, no. After the show.

EILEEN (*looks up*). Aren't you contracted?

ELLA. After this show. I'm getting out. I didn't think I really
    wanted to. But now I do.

MARIE. Well, ta-ra-ra-etcetera.

    Enter CHUB.

CHUB. Ella.

ELLA. Yes?

CHUB. It's nearly time.

MARIE. Get out. You see we're ready. So get out.

CHUB. The Colonel said –

    EILEEN *stops*.

EILEEN. I should have said Fuck Off. I should have told him. To
    his face.

MARIE. And where's the point in that?

CHUB. Ella.

    EILEEN *stands, goes behind the screen.* MARIE *goes to her table,
    powders her face.*

ELLA. Yes?

CHUB. Can I have a word. In private.

ELLA. No.

EILEEN *re-enters with a big little-girl hair-bow. She kneels to fix it in her hair.*

CHUB. It's important.

ELLA. You can tell me now.

CHUB. It's what the Colonel said.

EILEEN *and* MARIE *look at* CHUB.

ELLA. Yes?

CHUB. I didn't want to say this in front of everyone else. I shan't say it now.

ELLA. Come *on.*

CHUB. I know you don't look on me kindly. You'll look on me even less kindly.

ELLA. Yes?

CHUB. Alex has decided to sack Eileen and Marie. After today. He thinks they're sluts, and lower the tone of the performance.

Pause.

ELLA. What about me?

CHUB. He thinks you're chic. He likes your accent. He says that you've got class.

Pause.

Asked me to break the news. He said just to tell you, but you wouldn't let me.

Pause.

He's bringing in two new girls. Not been seen before. One of them lives with him.

MARIE. Lives with him?

ELLA. Oh, but you're the model of diplomacy –

CHUB. That's what I had to say. Two minutes.

He sits on the day-bed.

And he said to stay, and see that you were ready. Sorry, Eileen and Marie.

Pause. The WOMEN *are still.*

EILEEN. I knew it.

CHUB *takes a sado-sexmag from his pocket and reads it.*

CHUB. Let them weep, he said. What difference does it make.

EILEEN. The bugger's going to throw me out. I knew it.

She flings the teddy-bear at the radio. Pause. MARIE *goes to the radio, picks it up, sits, as she speaks.*

MARIE. Last month, I was seen in Dean Street, in a club, performing. By some bloke. He saw me afterwards. Come to my office, Friday. So I did. He said, I've got this show I'm bringing in. A funny show. I'd like you in it. So I said, well, yes, that's wonderful, what is it? Well, he said, the thing's a kind of satire, on the sexploit boom. It's called A Deeper Throat. What do I do, I said. Well, he said, don't worry, you don't have to sing or act or anything, just do your thing, 'cos that did get my nuts off, did your thing, so sparky, spiky, quirky, spry. I said Fuck Off. So angry that – I'd fallen for – the I-can-really-make-it bit . . . For which, in others, I'd reserved such scorn. And he said, well, a year ago, I would have said, that doesn't matter, 'cos there's hundreds more like you. But now it's different. Now there's thousands more like you.

Pause. Shrugs.

We must go on.

EILEEN (*goes and sits on the floor next to* MARIE, *picking up her teddy-bear*). I, um. There's this big mirror, in our bedroom. We like, well, he likes, no, I like as well, to, you know, sometimes, watch us, at it, in it. And when, last night, he, he was hitting me, about the legs and chest, I caught a glimpse of what was happening, I caught sight in the mirror of, me, being beaten up. And thought. Eh, look at that. You know, I think that someone ought to stop him doing that.

Pause. Shrugs.

We got to keep on working.

ELLA (*moving to stand behind* MARIE, *hand on her shoulder, to form a pleasing tableau, as she speaks*). I went to see a play, at the Old Vic Theatre. It was written 60 years ago, this play, but it was,

highly topical, about some national crisis, then. And everyone
was talking like they're talking now, no leaders, drift, despair.
And at the very end, these bombs came down, and nearly
killed the people. And they were sad, the bombs had missed.
And that seemed odd. And yet, the audience, who were all
people like these people, middle-class, and rich, and saying
just the same, about the crisis, still they clapped and clapped.
They surely didn't want a bomb on them. But what they said,
about the crisis, now, and what they saw, it didn't seem to fit.
Connect. As if, they couldn't see what they were watching.
Now, it's coming. So the experts say. Collapse of money.
National bankruptcy. Food riots. Barricades. Mob rule.

Pause.

I just don't know.

CHUB (*looks up from his magazine*). Don't read the papers much,
   myself.

MARIE (*angry*). Then LISTEN.

*She turns up the radio, loud. The last three words of the Archers intro,
followed by the theme tune and a word or two of dialogue.* MARIE
switches off the radio.

ELLA. Just don't know.

EILEEN (*stands*). Well, shall we go?

MARIE (*stands, briskly*). Let's go.

> MARIE *and* EILEEN *exit.* ELLA *exits.* CHUB *puts his magazine
> in his pocket and stands.*
> *Blackout and with it music: Suzi Quattro. Then lights on a tatty
> curtain. Possibly, crudely painted on it, a classical image, The Three
> Graces.*
> *The record stops in mid-phrase and starts again.*
> *Lights on the curtain change.*
> CHUB *to a microphone at the side.* ALEX *comes and sits in the
> audience. The record jumps, lights change again and then the record
> cuts out and blackout. In the darkness, curtains open.*
> *Music: Holst's 'Jupiter'.*
> *Lights on the three* WOMEN, *centre, in the same position as the
> tableau at the end of the last scene.*
> *Behind them is a mirror, as a back-drop, so we can see ourselves
> watching the* WOMEN, *who go into their act, to the Holst. They break*

from the tableau, one by one, and go into their act.

CHUB *starts reading something, very quickly. At first we can't hear the words, but gradually they become clear, grow louder and louder. During this, lights come up on the audience, so that, by the end, we see ourselves, in the mirror, and* WOMEN *are just silhouettes against it.*

CHUB. The Government returned to office on a national mandate to unite a bitterly divided people. Our record in fulfilling more speedily, more completely, than any other Government in history, the pledges we had made; this has entitled us to ask for a corresponding commitment, for a response no less total. The issue now is not whether this Government can survive, and lead the nation to full employment and a greater measure of social justice. It is whether any Government so constituted, so dedicated to the principles of consent and consensus within our democracy, can lead this nation. What the Government is asking for the year ahead, what the Government has the right to ask, the duty to ask, is not a year for self, but a year for Britain.

Cut out music and snap blackout.

End of play.

Connect, only connect
Howard's End

THE MIDAS CONNECTION

Characters

JACK
DUDLEY
VIC
NICK
EMMA
SHIFT WORKER
BANKERS

The Midas Connection was broadcast as part of the BBC series
Eleventh Hour, on 2 August 1975. The cast was as follows:

JACK	James Warrior
DUDLEY	Paul Copley
VIC	Barry Jackson
NICK	Edward Petherbridge
EMMA	Angela Scouler
SHIFT WORKER	Harry Davis
BANKERS	(Michael Barrington
	(John Carlin
	(Dennis Chinnery
	(Myles Hoyle
	(Richard Wardale

Directed by Mike Newell
Produced by Graeme McDonald

Although written for television, *The Midas Connection* could be
performed on stage. In a stage version, scene two (Nick's office)
would be cut, and scenes one and five (the Fixing Room) sound-
taped. The part of the Day-Shift Man could be doubled with Nick.

Scene One

The Fix Room.

ROTHSCHILD, MONTAGU, MATTHEY, MOCATTA *and*
SHARPS *at tables with telephones and little union flags on stands.*

ROTHSCHILD. Right, gentlemen, let's start at 172¾.

OTHERS (*variously, down their 'phones*). 72 and three start, starting
   at 72 and three . . .

SHARPS. Sharps is a buyer.

OTHERS (*variously, down 'phones*). Sharps is a buyer, Sharps buying.

MOCATTA. Mocatta selling.

OTHERS. Mocatta selling, Mocatta is a seller.

ROTHSCHILD. Rothschild have no interest.

OTHERS. Rothschild no interest, no interest Rothschild.

MATTHEY. Matthey buyer.

OTHERS. Matthey buying, Matthey buyer.

MONTAGU. Montagu buyer.

OTHERS. Montagu buying, Montagu's a buyer.

MATTHEY. Flag Matthey.

OTHERS. Matthey's flagged, flag Matthey.

MATTHEY. Flag down, Matthey no change.

OTHERS. Matthey no change, Matthey flag down no change.

ROTHSCHILD. Figures please.

OTHERS. Figures called.

MATTHEY. Matthey take 80 bars.

OTHERS. Matthey want 80, Matthey taking 80.

MONTAGU. Montagu want 60.

OTHERS. Montagu want 60, Montagu taking 60.

ROTHSCHILD. Rothschild now a buyer.

SHARPS. Sharps take 50.

OTHERS. Rothschild buying Sharps take 50, Rothschild is a buyer. Sharps want 50.

ROTHSCHILD. Rothschild want 60.

OTHERS. Rothschild taking 60, Rothschild want 60.

MOCATTA. Mocatta offer 10, Mocatta 10 to sell.

ROTHSCHILD. 250 wanted to 10 offered. Let's have a look at 174½, gentlemen.

MATTHEY. Flag Matthey.

OTHERS. Three and a half Matthey's flagged. Up to three half flag Matthey.

MATTHEY. Flag down, Matthey buys.

OTHERS. Matthey buying. Matthey's a buyer.

SHARPS. Flag Sharps.

Fade sound of fix.

VOICE OVER . This ritual occurs twice every weekday, at 10.30 am and 3 pm, in the offices of a merchant bank in the City of London. The participants are dealers, and they are fixing the world yardstick price of their commodity. At the beginning of the Fix, the Chairman of the dealers suggests a starting price. The dealers are in constant touch with their offices by telephone, and if a new buyer or seller comes on to the market, they stop the process of the Fix by raising a small Union Jack in front of them. The Fix is concluded when a price is offered to the dealers that attracts an equal number of buyers and sellers. The customers these men are dealing for are private individuals, banks, financial institutions, companies and even states. The commodity they are dealing in is gold.

While the above is happening, the fix soundlessly continues, again with each statement being repeated by the others, variously, down their telephones.

SHARPS. Down flag, Sharps buyer.

MATTHEY. Matthey a buyer.

ROTHSCHILD. Rothschild buying.

MATTHEY. Flag Matthey. Matthey no change.

MONTAGU. Montagu buyer.

MOCATTA. Mocatta buying.

ROTHSCHILD. No sellers. Let's try 176¾ gentlemen.

MOCATTA. Mocatta seller.

ROTHSCHILD. Rothschild seller.

MATTHEY. Matthey buyer.

SHARPS. Sharps buyer.

VOICE OVER *should stop about here, sound back in on fix.*

MATTHEY. Flag Matthey. Flag down Matthey no change.

MONTAGU. Montagu buyer.

ROTHSCHILD. Figures please.

MONTAGU. Montagu wants ten.

MOCATTA. Mocatta offer 20.

ROTHSCHILD. Rothschild offer 40.

MATTHEY. Matthey wants 60.

SHARPS. Sharps want 10.

MATTHEY. Flag Matthey. Flag down. Matthey down to 40.

ROTHSCHILD. 60 offered, 60 wanted, gentlemen, we fix at
     176¾.

OTHERS. Fixing at 176¾.

Scene Two

Corner of NICK's office.

     NICK *in shirtsleeves on the telephone.*

NICK (*hand over 'phone, calls*). Fixed at six and three.

> *Puts down 'phone.*

> (*To himself.*) Up four dollars, Bloody Hell.

Scene Three

The Fix Room.

The FIXERS *stand to leave.*

Scene Four

The vault.

DUDLEY *reading glossy sex magazine showing a girl dressed in gold jewellery.* DUDLEY *is sitting in an area of a gold vault, comprising a table, a few comfortable but unmatching chairs, piles of newspapers and magazines, tea mugs etc. A kettle somewhere. A little away a public telephone. Beyond the area the vaults themselves stretch away.* DUDLEY *tosses the magazine on to the table. He looks nervous. He takes a pay packet from his pocket, looks at the money, shakes his head.*

> *At the entrance of the vault* JACK, *mid 30's, is accepting some pieces of print-out from another man who is obviously leaving.*

JACK. Right then. That's 20,000 still owing from A613 and 4,000 owing to D300. And G63 needs another 6,000 to go out.

DAY-SHIFT MAN (*pointing to another list*). And that lot as well . . .

JACK. Oh, blimey.

DAY-SHIFT MAN. Well, you got all night.

JACK. It's supposed to be quiet. According to the Financial World Tonight the market is in a state of nervous inertia.

DAY-SHIFT MAN. You shouldn't believe everything you hear on the radio. There's something in the wind.

JACK. Like what?

DAY-SHIFT MAN (*shrugs*). Russians. Bound to be something to do with Russians.

Sniffs.

There's a lot on the move, anyway. Getting very bullish.

JACK. Well, bully for it.

DAY-SHIFT MAN. Have a nice night.

JACK. Ta, very much.

DAY-SHIFT MAN *walks off.*

DUDLEY *is still smoking. He stands, goes to the 'phone, lifts it, thinks better of it, puts it down. Sits, picks up the* Daily Express.

VIC *is at a shelf. Above the shelf a sign,* P113. VIC *is piling gold from a trolley on to the shelf.*

JACK *enters.*

JACK. Vic?

DUDLEY. Down among the Ps.

JACK. Come on. Heavy night.

DUDLEY. Right I'll – be just a minute, okay.

JACK. Don't take all night.

JACK *leaves.* DUDLEY *stands to 'phone, rings a number.*

DUDLEY. Hello, Petal. Me. Look, had you thought of your smashing aunt? (*Pause.*) Oh. (*Pause.*) Old boot. (*Pause,*) What? No. (*Puts the 'phone down and turns to go.*)

JACK *is now helping* VIC.

JACK. Apparently some Italian jewellers, to recycle the flecks of gold they lose in production, burn their own floorboards. Makes you think.

VIC. Three quid short this week.

JACK. Used to do it in the vaults here too, but they found the new floor was more expensive than the gold they got back.

VIC. Something to do with superannuation.

JACK. I read that in Japan there's this hotel with this solid gold bath and people pay 1,000 yen to go and sit in it. Supposed to add three years to your life.

VIC. Hey, have you ever thought of entering for Mastermind?

JACK. I like to know a bit about my work.

VIC. I'd like to know a bit more about my pay.

JACK. Eh, what happened today? Pricewise?

VIC. Went up. Why?

JACK. Something in the wind, Harry said. Something about the Russians.

VIC. The Russians? They're selling. To pay for grain. 8½ thousand to P113 for starters.

JACK (*puzzled*). Oh, I thought he said it was bullish. More buyers. Perhaps –

DUDLEY *appears*.

VIC. Well done, we've just finished.

JACK. There's a lot need weighing.

DUDLEY. Right.

They walk to the weighing machine. They weigh a pile of gold bars in lots.

VIC. I remember with a great deal of delight when I was in weaving.

JACK. Yes?

VIC. You'd stand watching your machine – a Dobcross or a Hattersley, the warp and the weft knitting together as the spindle shot across, the whole thing juddering and jostling, and at the end out comes the cloth. I mean the chap was just keeping an eye on it, nothing particularly interesting about it, but just seeing that cloth come out and very occasionally, well hardly ever, well sometimes, you'd see that cloth or not that cloth, but something similar, a similar pattern, on someone's back in the street. D'you see what I mean?

Pause.

Now, what are we doing? Humping hunks of metal about. Alienated from my product, I am.

DUDLEY. Were you in weaving? I was in finishing.

VIC. Where?

DUDLEY. Bradford. Where were you?

VIC. Halifax. (*Pause.*) Why d'you come South?

DUDLEY. You know. I went to the Midlands first. Safe as houses. Workshop of the world. If you can't get a job in the Midlands, you can't get a job anywhere. Cast iron.

VIC. Where d'you work?

DUDLEY. British Leyland.

VIC. Ah.

JACK. Eh. Have you heard the one about the Aston Villa goalie who fell under a 'bus?

DUDLEY. No?

JACK. It's all right it went straight through his legs.

DUDLEY. They're in the first division now.

VIC. You're earning a damn sight less, I bet.

JACK. Well, at least this job's secure.

DUDLEY. Money.

The job is finished.

VIC. Right.

DUDLEY (*of the gold they have weighed*). Is this going anywhere?

JACK. A613 is where it's going, sunbeam.

DUDLEY. Bit silly i'n'it, really. Just moving it about, pile to pile.

VIC (*humping the weighed gold on to a trolley*). They dig it out of deep holes in distant parts. They ship it here and rebury it in other deep holes specially constructed for the purpose. Lunatic. As Lenin himself says –

JACK. Oh, yeah.

VIC. – after the revolution the only use for this stuff'll be for paving public lavatories. Useless you see.

JACK. Keeps them happy.

DUDLEY. Keep 'em off the streets.

They pile the gold on to an empty shelf on which they stack it.

VIC. Now there you're wrong. In 1925 Winston Churchill put
Britain back on the Gold Standard. All they did, transferred
some of this from one pile to another in the Bank of
England; Pile I England to Pile II France, and because of
that, they had to print less pound notes, and because of that
the mine owners imposed a wage cut and because of that
there was a general strike.

JACK (*to* DUDLEY). I blame myself really.

VIC. Eh?

JACK. For Vic's condition.

DUDLEY. What do you mean?

JACK. I mean, it all started innocently enough. He'd been picking
up the *Morning Star* outside Moorgate tube station, you know,
not every day, just occasionally, just feeling sorry for the poor
girl selling it.

VIC. Very droll.

JACK. And I suppose it was inevitable, really, that, you know,
he'd want a bit of background, go into it deeper, and he went
into pamphlets, nothing strong, you know, just the occasional
bulletin of the Committee to Release the Shrewsbury
whatever and he seemed fine.

VIC. Yes, very humorous, Jack.

JACK. Of course, he claimed, even then, he could take it or leave
it alone, but I could tell that it was becoming a thing with
him, an insatiable urge, it went from bad to worse, he started
going on to the real hard-line stuff, you know, the
Grundrisse, Stalin on Philology. And then, one day, he
finished *Das Kapital* Vol. Two, and he wanted Vol. Three.
Well, they'd told him, at Hammersmith Public, it was out,
there was nothing they could do. But he went wild. He was
crawling around on the floor, just screaming for it, he
wouldn't listen, it was a terrible sight to behold. Hooked.

VIC. Hm.

DUDLEY. You shouldn't blame yourself.

VIC. Well, that's very inventive, Jack, very well articulated. I have to admire your –

An electronic sound.

DUDLEY. What's that?

JACK. It's the bloody telex, that's what that is.

VIC and JACK move out of shot. DUDLEY takes a piece of paper covered with scribbled calculations from his pocket, looks at it, then follows.

JACK and VIC at telex.

JACK. 12,000! Screaming Ada! This'll take all night!

Passage of time. Later.

DUDLEY and JACK are working, JACK consulting piece of print-out. VIC is making tea nearby.

JACK. I don't know where all this stuff's coming from. I mean, it shouldn't be coming down now at all. It's 2 a-bloody-m. That lot up there thinks it all moves by magic.

VIC. Tea?

JACK and DUDLEY to table area.

JACK. And there's some packaging.

VIC. You mean some of this stuff is actually moving, actually going somewhere?

JACK. Other banks, other vaults. Can't keep the stuff at home.

DUDLEY. How much is a fridge?

JACK. What do you want a fridge for at this time of night?

DUDLEY. I've got a fridge. I want to sell it.

JACK. Second-hand?

DUDLEY. Of course it's second-hand. It's in my hand.

JACK. Well, about £50, I suppose.

DUDLEY. Fifty . . . fifty.

He goes off to the phone.

VIC. What's up with him?

VIC *pours himself tea*.

JACK. Do you know the biggest importer of gold outside Europe is India, most of it smuggled? From Dubai. They fly it there quite legally, bullion dealers, British Airways flights, and then it gets turned into jewellery and the smugglers ship it into India.

VIC. How do they get away with it?

JACK. There's an awful lot of dentists in Dubai.

DUDLEY *re-appears*.

DUDLEY. We bloody rent it.

JACK. Rent what?

DUDLEY. The fridge. Whoever heard of renting a fridge?

JACK. Is it gas?

DUDLEY. I don't know.

JACK. You can rent gas fridges. It's more economical.

VIC. Why this sudden obsession with fridges?

DUDLEY. I've got a – I'm in a state of . . . um. Some financial embarrassment.

VIC. Payments on the fridge?

DUDLEY. No, not on the fridge. On the house. And the furniture. And my bike. And some running expenses that I finance through a loan, most particularly in fact, that loan. But no, so far as I was aware the fridge was about the only thing we are actually in the black on. That's why I thought of selling it.

Pause.

JACK. What you –

DUDLEY. You see, this loan – it isn't really a company, an official agency, it's more of a backstreet kind of loan, a loan-shark type of loan, and this guy, I borrowed it to pay back another loan, at rather higher interest, and he now, sort of wants it back.

Pause.

VIC. Is there anything we can . . .

DUDLEY. Well not unless you've got six hundred quid.

JACK. Oh blimey.

A 'phone, not the public 'phone, rings. VIC answers.

VIC. Hello. (*Pause.*) You'll want to talk to Mr Henderson.

JACK. Will he?

VIC. He will? We've got a visitor. (*He hands the 'phone to JACK.*)

JACK. Hello.

DUDLEY. Visitor?

JACK. What?

VIC. The Director of Overseas Finance.

DUDLEY. Why?

VIC. God alone knows.

JACK. Now? Oh, well, of course –

DUDLEY. What's he doing here at this time of night?

VIC. How should I know? Snooping.

JACK (*amazed. Putting 'phone down*). They are letting him in.

DUDLEY. Well, it *is* his bank.

VIC. It's our vault.

JACK walks to the door, shaking his head.

DUDLEY. I mean, who is he?

VIC. How should I know. He's a faceless financial mastermind.

DUDLEY. Better look busy.

JACK at the door.

NICK and EMMA appear from outside, in evening dress. EMMA wears gold earrings.

NICK. Hello.

JACK. Hello.

NICK. It's very good of you –

JACK. Oh not at all. Your bank.

NICK. Your vault.

> *A sticky pause.*

I'm Nick. And this is Emma.

JACK. Jack.

EMMA. How do you do.

> **DUDLEY** *and* **VIC** *appear.*

JACK. And this is Dudley and this is Vic. Nick. And, um –

EMMA. Emma.

JACK. Emma.

NICK. Hi.

DUDLEY. Hi.

VIC. How do you do.

> *Pause.*

NICK. Business brisk?

JACK. Oh, yes.

> *They all go into the table area silently.*

Um – is there anything – ?

NICK. Emma wanted to see a vault.

EMMA. Emma did not want to see a vault.

NICK (*to* DUDLEY). Er – anything come through tonight?

DUDLEY. Yeah, quite a lot.

NICK. May I – er – ?

> *They go to the teleprinter.*

> *Silence between* EMMA, NICK *and* DUDLEY.

JACK. Bullish.

NICK (*takes print-out*). Yes.

> *To* EMMA, *gesturing to the vault.*

Here it is.

EMMA. So it is. (*She wanders away.*)

VIC (*to* JACK). Right then, packaging.

NICK. Yes, please don't let me . . .

> EMMA *picks up a gold bar. She drops it. Clang.*

NICK. It's heavier than you think.

VIC. It is.

EMMA. I dropped it.

NICK. Four hundred Troy ounces, give or take a Troy.

VIC. Indeed.

JACK *goes and retrieves the bar, as* NICK *finishes the print-out and produces a half bottle of scotch.*

NICK. Look, would any of you lads like a drink?

> *Passage of time. Later.*
>
> DUDLEY, NICK *and* EMMA *are drinking.* JACK *and* VIC *are in the distance packaging some gold.*

NICK. You see, there are those who argue that gold should have no place in the monetary system at all. That it's a barbarous relic. But, you see, gold is in effect the only thing that has real value in itself. So people go for it. When there's a lack of – confidence – in paper currency. Confidence, the key.

> *Pause.*

It's been said with a lot of truth that governments decide what is legal tender, but the people decide what is money.

The French have always had a lot of confidence in gold. This is particularly because, I imagine, they've had little cause to have confidence in the franc. There is in fact twice the amount of gold in private hands, buried in the garden, under mattresses, as there is in the Bank of France.

Another?

DUDLEY. Thanks.

NICK. In England, of course, you can't hold bullion, but you can hold Krugerrands. Most of my gold's in Krugerrands.

EMMA (*singing*). 'A something, a something is quite sentimental, but Krugerrands are a girl's best friend . . . ' (*Laughs.*)

NICK. Gold sovereigns, ounce for ounce are a bit more pricey, but because they're still legal tender you don't pay tax on them, so it's six of one really . . . I'll stick to Krugerrands.

DUDLEY. Yuh.

EMMA. Patriotic bastard.

NICK. There is nothing nationalistic about gold. Anonymous, colourless, creedless, classless, as de Gaulle said, impartial and universal. The barometer of confidence in everything else.

VIC *and* JACK *approach.*

JACK. Fancy doing some work, Dudley?

DUDLEY. Oh yuh, I was just listening to –

VIC. So I noticed.

NICK. It's pleasant down here, isn't it?

EMMA. You must be joking.

NICK. Cool, I mean, not cold.

JACK. Air conditioned.

NICK. Yes. Would you like some more whisky?

JACK. Why not.

NICK. Love-ly.

They get their mugs. NICK *pours.*

That's it I'm afraid. Cheers.

They clink mugs.

EMMA. I have had a frightful evening. I have been surrounded by morbid merchant bankers and suicidal stockbrokers and nobody will tell me what is going on.

NICK (*factually*). Emma, you are about to fall over.

EMMA. Then I shall tell a joke about a merchant banker. Who had just completed a speculative coup. And he went on a luxury cruise on the proceeds of his triumph and fell overboard. And the entire ship's company watched in horror as this huge great shark swam towards him, this merchant banker, who was thrashing and spluttering. And then at the last moment, the shark turned away and the banker was saved. And someone asked why didn't the shark eat him. Didn't he like the look of him? No, someone else replied, professional etiquette.

All laugh like drains.

JACK. Isn't it wonderful that such a disparate group of people united only in their common bond, with an inert common metal, soluble in nitric and hydrochloric acid, melting at 1064.43° Centigrade, can still come together and break, break you know, together –

EMMA. Wind?

JACK. Bread.

EMMA. Wine, and bread. Come together and break wine together. Creedless, classless, impartial, universal and gummy with a monumental gloom.

She sits. Pause.

VIC. Gloomy? Who's gloomy? Are you gloomy Jack?

JACK. I'm not gloomy.

VIC. Neither am I.

EMMA (*of* NICK) He's gloomy.

Pause. NICK is reading print-out, not listening.

EMMA (*to* NICK, *conversationally*). If diamonds are a girl's best friend, I'm only here for de beer.

Pause.

NICK. You could presumably stay down here for months. The air conditioning.

JACK. Yes, if you wanted to.

Pause.

NICK. We'd better go.

JACK picks up 'phone. Dials.

JACK (*down 'phone*). They're coming out.

NICK. Come on Emma.

He helps her up.

EMMA. I want to have a Krugerrand.

NICK. You can't have a Krugerrand, Emma, (*To* JACK.) Thanks very much.

JACK. Oh, not at all. Thanks for the whisky.

NICK. My pleasure.

They go towards the door.

EMMA. I want to take a gold bar.

NICK. You can't take a gold bar, Emma.

They've gone.

VIC. I wonder why he came.

DUDLEY. She wanted to see a vault. He said. They'd been to some big do, sloshed out of her mind, she wanted to see some real gold.

Clanging of a door. Re-enter JACK.

Odd, she was wearing enough.

JACK. Came to look at it. Look at the vault. See it was still here.

VIC. There was something.

JACK. You what?

VIC. There was something. I don't know what. The eyes.

DUDLEY. Zonked out of her skull.

VIC. He came to check it out!

JACK. What?

VIC. The bastard.

DUDLEY. Who?

VIC. Him.

JACK. Why?

VIC (*suddenly very angry standing, walking towards the shelves*). Because he spends his days buying and selling this stuff, which you can't eat, or wear, or build houses of, just buy and sell and own, and for which people die, getting it out of the ground.

JACK. One for every two tons mined. Five hundred a year. 41.6 a month. 1.38 a day.

VIC. Today!

Pause – he looks at them.

Yes?

He strides into the vault.

JACK. Well, what was all that in aid of?

Passage of time. Later.

DUDLEY and VIC *are working at a shelf.* JACK *is in the distance.*

DUDLEY. He seemed apologetic to me.

VIC. Well, he's got enough to apologise for.

DUDLEY. Why you get so lathered up about it?

VIC. You know Jack, he used to make motor bikes. He was very fond of motor bikes. He doesn't talk about them that much now, that's all. (*Pause.*) Look. Money. Start of money. Blokes. You. Making bread. I. Bakery. You make five loaves.

He lays out five gold bars.

One . . . two . . . three . . . four . . . five. And I pay you five quid.

He puts a pound from his wallet on each bar.

But I don't charge a quid a piece for the loaves. I charge £1.25 for my loaves, so you, with your wages, can only buy four back. And I keep the other loaf, and eat it. And I employ another baker and I've two loaves over and then another two and I've got four loaves, and there's a limit to the amount even I can eat, so I sell them, and I keep the cash. And on, up and up the scale, loaf upon loaf, making, pocketing the difference between what I pay and what I make. But there comes a point, and now we're not just talking about the loaves, when you and millions of others, have made all the things people need, food, clothes, houses, cars, energy, all those things. There comes a point, there's always a point, when you can't afford to buy them back.

He picks up a gold bar.

You can't buy them because we have taken the money you could use to buy it away from you. And then, unless we do something magic, we have to stop paying you, wait a while until we can eat up all the extra loaves and have a slump. A great depression. So, do something magic.

Slight pause.

DUDLEY. Inflation. If you haven't got the money, you, to spend, to buy back all the things you've made . . .

VIC. Invent it. Credit. Loans. The printing press. Print toy-town money. Tons of it. But all you're doing, staving off. Then, slump. And each slump deeper down.

Pause.

So they go on printing, and it's not worth a thing. A huge inverted pyramid resting on a tiny speck of real value, gold. And all the rest is confidence.

DUDLEY. Just confidence.

JACK *appears.*

JACK. Hello, Lenin.

A 'phone rings.

VIC. That's the 'phone, Jack.

JACK. Who'd be ringing now, it's 6.00 am.

DUDLEY. Perhaps the lira's collapsed.

VIC. Perhaps the pound's collapsed.

JACK. It's the public 'phone.

DUDLEY. Eh?

JACK. It's the public 'phone.

Suddenly DUDLEY rushes to the 'phone and picks it up. The others follow.

DUDLEY. Yuh? (*Pause.*) Oh Christ. When? (*Pause.*) Well, aren't
they charmers? Aren't they bloody charmers? (*Pause.*) Yuh.
Nine o'clock. (*Pause.*) Don't worry.

He puts the 'phone down.

What a bloody stupid thing to say.

JACK. What?

DUDLEY. Don't worry.

VIC. What's up?

Pause – DUDLEY sits.

DUDLEY. They rang her up. I mean, now, five minutes ago.
People from – the loan person. Said they knew, you know, I
worked nights and they'd be popping round. Tonight.
Tomorrow morning, 1.00 am. When they knew I'd be at
work, to pick up the loan and interest . . .

Pause.

Sod it. Six hundred quid.

VIC. Don't pay it. Get together. Few of your mates. Us, maybe.
Sort the bastards out. All you need's the confidence to do it.

DUDLEY. Yuh.

VIC *notices a gold earring on the floor. He picks it up, places it on the
table in some triumph.*

VIC. Her very own nugget. They'll be back.

Passage of time. Later.

Rediscover VIC *at door admitting* NICK, *in business suit, and*
EMMA, *also in day clothes.*

NICK. Earring. She left an earring.

EMMA. It must be here somewhere.

VIC. Well, let's have a look.

As they walk towards the table area.

NICK. Emma wanted, she wanted to be sure before you went off
the shift.

EMMA. It's an heirloom.

NICK. You haven't spotted – ?

VIC (*picking up the earring from the table*). Safe and sound.

EMMA. Thank God for that.

NICK. You see? I told you, safe, here, has to be.

EMMA. Thank God.

> EMMA *picks up the earring, goes off towards the door.* NICK *taking his wallet from his pocket.*

NICK. Look –

> VIC *shakes his head.*

Thanks, anyway.

VIC. Oh, not at all.

> *Reaction of* JACK *and* DUDLEY *as* NICK *and* EMMA *leave.* VIC *comes back in.*

What about that?

DUDLEY. Panic. In his eyes.

VIC. Blind panic. (*Slight pause.*)

What was the gold price yesterday?

JACK. I don't know. Up. Been going up for weeks.

VIC. And the Russians are selling gold.

JACK. What?

VIC. Bad harvest. Need to sell to pay for grain. The Russians are *selling* gold. So the price should fall. So why's it going up?

JACK. Well, I just move the stuff.

VIC. Because somewhere there's a panic. Don't know where. Somewhere, in the world, some economy, some currency, some multi-national company, some market, some institution on which the value of a paper currency depends, is troubled. Anonymously. Just a number. Secretly. But deeply. And they don't know which. They don't know when. So – panic. And so he comes down here. To look at it. Because it's safe. Eye up the place – check it out. It's isolated. It's impregnable. It's air conditioned. Bolt-hole. For the day when every other bolt-hole is closed.

DUDLEY. Collapse of confidence. The pyramid.

VIC. Exactly.

JACK. Come on, Vic. It's nearly knocking off time.

VIC. Somewhere a crisis, lurking. And they don't know where.

DUDLEY. And then the lavatories will all be paved with gold?

VIC (*gesturing around*). The biggest public pisshouse in the world. Gilt edged graffiti. Eighteen carat cubicles. Soft, gentle, double-ply rolled gold. I'm off to spend a Krugerrand.

He strides off.

JACK (*looking at his watch*). Another day.

VIC (*shouts from afar*). It's confidence, you see. They haven't got any, young Dud, they haven't got any

DUDLEY. Fool's gold.

Scene Five

The Fix Room. 10.30 am

The same as first sequence, but this time, an undefined feeling of genteel panic – again all lines repeated down the telephone.

ROTHSCHILD. Right, gentlemen, let's start at 180. Rothschild's a buyer.

MATTHEY. Matthey buying.

MONTAGU. Montagu's a buyer.

MOCATTA. Mocatta buyer.

MATTHEY. Flag Matthey. Matthey no change.

SHARPS. Sharps buying.

ROTHSCHILD. No sellers. 181.

SHARPS. Sharps buying.

ROTHSCHILD. Rothschild buying.

MOCATTA. Mocatta selling.

MATTHEY. Matthey buying.

MONTAGU. Montagu buying.

MOCATTA. Flag Mocatta. Mocatta now a buyer.

ROTHSCHILD. No sellers. Let's try 182.

SHARPS. Sharps buying.

ROTHSCHILD. Rothschild's a buyer at 182 . . .

End of play.